APEX PREDATOR
THE UNTOLD TRUTH BEHIND MARRIAGE

Decoding Relationships in a World of Convenience and Compromise

By Pheladi Anastacia Thaba

Apex Predator: The Untold Truth Behind Marriage

Copyright © 2025 by Pheladi Anastacia Thaba.

All rights reserved. No part of this publication may be reproduced, distributed, or transmitted in any form or by any means, including photocopying, recording, or other electronic or mechanical methods without the prior written permission of the author except in the case of brief quotations embodied in reviews and certain other non-commercial uses permitted by copyright law.

Published by
Brookscraft Publishing
A Division of Brooks Craft LLC
Info@brookscraftpublishing.com
www.brookscraftpublishing.com

Author's Contact

To book the author as a speaker at your next event or to order bulk copies of this book, please, use the email below:

anikiepheladi2@gmail.com

Dedication

To all women and men who have been told to sit down and be quiet. And to those who stood up anyway.

Most of all to my late dad who never yielded, argued or laid a hand to my mum. P.S. Madimetja Daniel Thaba continue to Rest in Peace.

My dad once said

"It's easier to build strong children than it is to repair weak men".

About the Author

Pheladi Anastacia Thaba, the visionary entrepreneur behind Medim8s Pty Ltd, is on a mission to empower individuals and create a lasting impact. From overcoming challenges as a foreigner to establishing a thriving business, Pheladi's journey exemplifies determination and strong focus on human beauty by transforming lives through life coaching and mindset. Pheladi emphasizes the importance of persistence and a growth mindset. She believes that challenges indicate being on the right path, while adjustments are needed to keep pushing boundaries.

Pheladi Anastacia Thaba is a mother of one and wife with marriage experience. Her journey from the foreign land of South Africa become a successful businesswoman in Australia is an inspiration for dreamers and visionaries. Her determination, resilience, and strategic marketing showcase the power of entrepreneurship.

It is possible for anyone to overcome the impossible. I will continue to empower individuals and unlock their true potential in all aspects of life, from self-love, to confidence and to stating the untold truth about us as living creatures.

Love alone isn't enough to hold a marriage together! (Marriage Act 1836 and 1949)

Table of Contents

Dedication iii

Table of Contents v

Introduction 6

The Marriage Mirage 8

Love vs. Convenience 29

The Statistics Speak 48

The Psychology of Love 67

Red Flags and Early Signs 89

Real Stories, Real Lessons 110

Building Authentic Connections 131

The Role of Communication 153

Navigating Compromise 174

The Future of Marriage 195

Empowerment Through Knowledge 212

Thanks for Joining the Ride! 232

Introduction

Hey there, Wonderful Reader!

Alright, let's get real for a moment. We live in a world where the concept of marriage can feel like a mirage—beautifully enticing but often out of reach. This book? It's all about pulling back the curtain on the hidden motivations behind modern marriages. You might be wondering, what inspired this romp through the labyrinth of love and commitment? Well, buckle up, because we're diving deep into the why's and how behind the most universal yet complex human experience is! From the start, my goal has been to uncover the underlying forces at play in our relationships, to shake up the misconceptions that keep us stuck, and to challenge the norms that might hold us hostage. You'll find that this isn't just a book filled with dry statistics; it's a lively recipe—sprinkled with juicy real-life stories, research gems, and practical tips that will empower you to nurture genuine love in your own life.

As I poured over mountains of research and listened to countless personal narratives, I was struck by the shocking revelations of how societal pressures and personal histories shape our views on love. It was a wild ride—to see how often convenience and practical considerations overshadow heartfelt affection! Chapters like "The Marriage Mirage" and "Love vs. Convenience" don't just dissect the illusions we subscribe to but also encourage you to think critically about what drives you and your partner's choices. And trust me, this isn't just your typical relationship manual. The book is structured in thematic sections, each offering tools and insights that challenge you to reflect on your own life. Yes, I want you flipping the pages with that burning curiosity, eager to examine your own experiences in light of what's revealed.

But it's not just about discovering the raw truths; it's also about forging connections! "Building Authentic Connections" offers down-to-earth advice on nurturing those meaningful relationships we all crave. You'll learn how to keep the flame alive—not just with your partner, but with yourself. I want you to wield the power of knowledge, to engage in open dialogues, and to navigate the nuanced art of compromise without losing your incredible self! This journey is about you taking the reins, shifting from passive acceptance to active participation in your relationship narrative.

I truly believe that understanding the psychology of love can revolutionize how we experience it. This book invites you not just to read but to reflect and act—to become your own advocate for a fulfilling partnership. Each chapter ends with thought-provoking questions and actionable insights to ensure you don't just skim through, but dive in headfirst! Oh, and let me warn you, some parts might challenge you to rethink long-held beliefs about love and marriage. But that's the beauty of it!

So, are you ready to engage with the nuances of this ever-evolving landscape of relationships? It's time to peel back the layers, challenge the status quo, and embark on a journey that may transform your understanding of love from a fantasy into a lived reality. I can't wait for you to start this joyous adventure with me and ultimately, to discover nuggets of wisdom that resonate and inspire change in your own life. Stick with me until the end—I promise it will be worth it. You've got this!

Cheers to love and growth, **Pheladi Anastacia Thaba**

The Marriage Mirage

Unveiling the Illusions

The notion of marriage has been romanticized to an extent that it often bears little resemblance to the challenging reality many couples face. Society, bolstered by media portrayals, cultural narratives, and age-old traditions, offers a view of marriage that typically reflects unswerving bliss, eternal love, and unending partnership. This idealized depiction can create expectations that are not only unrealistic but also incredibly damaging, steering individuals toward hasty decisions based on a fantasy rather than an informed understanding of what marriage truly entails.

Consider the fairy tales that dominate children's literature, where love is often equated with a one-time magical moment that culminates in a wedding. These narratives imply that achieving that "happily ever after" is merely about getting to the altar, creating an illusion that life's complexities dissipate once the vows are exchanged. As adults, we are often bombarded with similar depictions in romantic comedies, where conflicts are resolved within the span of a few witty exchanges, and real-life struggles are glossed over in favor of an enchanting conclusion. The pervasive influence of these narratives contributes to a seductive, yet flawed, understanding of what a successful marriage looks like.

Such illusions shape our expectations to the point that many enter marriage without a clear comprehension of what it involves. Rather than viewing marriage as a partnership that requires ongoing effort, communication, and commitment, they are often fixated on the ceremonious aspects and a symbol of love—a ring or wedding dress—believing these objects will imbue their union with significance. When the realities of marital life, which may include financial strain, life changes, and differing personal goals, set in, many find themselves unprepared for the emotional turbulence of everyday life.

To grasp this disparity between reality and expectation, let's delve deeper into the narratives we encounter daily. Media narratives shape our beliefs and perceptions about romance and relationship dynamics. They deliver stories in digestible snippets, promoting a sanitized version of love that often disregards the nuances inherent in long-term partnerships. When we engage in conversations with couples, we often uncover hidden challenges that starkly contrast with the sugar-coated portrayals of relationships. For instance, in one interview, Sarah and Tom, married for eight years, recounted how they initially adored the idea of marriage, enamored by the sparkle of their wedding day. However, they admitted that the pressures of career competition, differing aspirations, and unresolved conflicts led them to experience a profound sense of disillusionment. "We thought we'd ride off into the sunset after the ceremony," Sarah reflected. "It wasn't until later that we realized the sunset is just another part of life and doesn't magically solve everything."

Such testimonials abound, revealing a consistent theme: the sentiment that their marriage, viewed through the lens of media and societal expectations, was far less glamorous than advertised. This frequent misalignment can have serious psychological impacts. Couples may find themselves struggling under the burden of those unfulfilled expectations. When relationships falter—settling into the everyday rhythms that don't match the excitement of what was portrayed—they often feel a sense of failure. The culture of comparison further amplifies these feelings. With social media inundating our lives with meticulously curated snapshots of other people's "perfect" marriages, the outcome is an internal dialogue that whispers incessantly, "Why isn't our marriage like that?" As a result, this illusion creates a toxic cycle: individuals feel pressure to maintain a façade of happiness and success, even as they grapple with their own discontent.

Now, let's introduce a pivotal voice in our exploration: The Researcher, a psychological analyst dedicated to studying the impact of societal myths on personal relationships. The Researcher expresses concern over the neat packaging of marriage ideals devoid of context. "Many couples enter marriage with inflated notions of love," they explain. "They expect to be constantly fulfilled and blissfully happy, which is unrealistic because love itself isn't static; it's dynamic, evolving through life's ebbs and flows." This wisdom prompts further examination of the illusion of perpetual love.

The Researcher's insights help to lay bare the ramifications of these misconceptions. Through thorough research—surveys, psychological evaluations, and interviews with numerous couples—they have uncovered alarming statistics: over 70% of individuals, regardless of age, reported that their understanding of marriage has been heavily influenced by media portrayals, leading to mismatched expectations when they enter into it. This statistic opens a conversation about how such narratives contribute not only to personal disappointment but also more broadly to societal patterns—patterns that might perpetuate the cycle of divorce and emotional dysfunction.

In tandem with these insights, we can begin to grasp how love and commitment are often influenced by other underlying factors, such as financial security, social status, and cultural expectations. In examining the motivations driving many toward marriage, it becomes evident that while love is an element, it's often not the sole factor at play. Mel, a newly married young woman, articulated this struggle when she reflected on her peers' relationships, saying, "Sometimes I feel like I married my husband not just because I love him but because it felt like the expected next step, like checking a box." This sentiment underscores the reality that many decisions surrounding marriage lack clear roots in authentic connection.

Moreover, we have a pair of illustrative case studies that highlight the tension between the ideal and the real. One couple, Jenna and Alex, rushed their decision to marry merely after a year of dating after feeling societal pressure from friends and family. "Everyone expected us to take that leap," Jenna shared. "We were told you have to marry at a certain age—so we did." Upon reflection, both shared how the joyous expectations of marriage faded when confronted with shared financial responsibilities and their differing views on parenting. "We realized too late that we didn't fully know each other," Jenna lamented, "and that's where the real challenges began."

In an opposite scenario, we find Lisa and Marc, who chose to marry after eight years of deep friendship and commitment. They took their time to understand each other's values, needs, and boundaries before making that lifelong commitment. "Our relationship was built on a strong foundation of trust and friendship," Lisa notes. "We knew that marriage wouldn't be the end of our struggles but rather an indication that we were ready to confront them together." Their approach signifies a vital truth that often eludes couples caught in the thrill of romance—the acknowledgment that compatibility and commitment take work.

Through these contrasting narratives, we can see that those who enter marriage based on societal pressure or romanticized expectations often encounter greater disillusionment. Emotionally and psychologically, the disappointment can lead to a cascade of issues: low self-esteem, resentment toward one's partner, and even prolonged unhappiness in a partnership that no longer seems aligned with personal aspirations. These experiences elucidate the sobering reality that, while the wedding day may symbolize union, it does not protect against the complexities that surface in day-to-day life.

The burden of societal expectations often weighs heavily on individuals, leading many to forge paths in marriage that might conflict with their sense of self or happiness. This disparity between the idealized version of marriage promoted by culture and the complexities of relational dynamics can foster a toxic environment—both within marriages and in society. Indeed, the pressure to conform leaves little space for individuality, innovation, or the authentic connection that sustains relationships through trial and time.

The myths surrounding marriage don't merely cause disappointment; they can have far-reaching psychological implications, steering people away from the authentic connections they crave. The Researcher's hypotheses enhance our understanding of this phenomenon, suggesting that the dream of a "perfect marriage" can lead to feelings of inadequacy and alienation. As these misconceptions bubble beneath the surface of marital life, many struggle to discern what genuine love looks like, often mistaking a fleeting infatuation for enduring affection.

Engaging with experts in the field, The Researcher considers how these myths can be dismantled. They advocate for narratives that focus on truthfulness and vulnerability in relationships, encouraging couples to step beyond romantic clichés. Meaningful conversations surrounding the realities of marriage—those that include discussions about financial responsibilities, shared ambitions, emotional labor, and life's unpredictability—can cultivate resilience within partnerships.

As individuals begin to recognize and challenge the illusions surrounding marriage, moreover, there exists an opportunity for profound personal growth. By willingly confronting the myths that seduced them into taking the plunge, individuals can gain the clarity needed to build sincere and fulfilling relationships. This practice of critical reflection not only promotes self-awareness but empowers individuals to enter unions where love and companionship flourish beyond the gilded edges of societal expectations.

Moving forward, we would benefit from fostering dialogue about what marriage must realistically encompass. Engaging deeply with the shared truths and vulnerabilities inherent in partnership can anchor relationships amid life's upheaval. With intention and commitment to fostering authentic connections, can marriage morph from the mirage it once seemed into a fulfilling, complex journey filled with growth, love, and cooperation?

In exploring the illusions of marriage and the psychological ramifications of these societal myths, we can shed light on the ways in which the romanticized view of marriage is often a detriment to genuine connections. Understanding the impact of these illusions sets the stage for a deeper discussion about the foundations required to build healthy, authentic relationships—one grounded in truth, transparency, and a shared commitment to endure life's highs and lows in partnership. The time has come to unveil these illusions, for in doing so, we prepare individuals for a more honest, authentic experience of love and, ultimately, the journey of marriage.

Societal Expectations and Their Consequences

The notion of marriage has long been steeped in cultural norms and societal expectations, serving as a backdrop for how individuals perceive themselves and their relationships. From an early age, many are treated to a fairy tale version of matrimony—happy endings, grand ceremonies, and an eternal bond of love. Yet, as we venture into adulthood, the reality of marriage often diverges significantly from these idyllic depictions. This subchapter delves into the societal pressures surrounding marriage, discussing how cultural norms dictate what a successful marriage should look like, and highlighting the consequences of adhering to these ideals.

Marriage is often seen as the ultimate goal in a person's life, particularly within societies that value family structure and stability. To be married is not only a personal commitment to another person but also a public declaration of social status. These ideals can instill in individuals a sense of duty to conform to societal expectations, prioritizing the façade of a successful marriage over genuine emotional connection. This subchapter examines the intricate relationship between societal expectations, personal identity, and the lived realities of marriage, ultimately urging readers to question the narratives they have been taught.

One might explore the experiences of couples who feel the weight of these expectations. Consider Emily and Jake, who met in college and quickly fell in love. Eager to forge a life together, they felt compelled to marry shortly after graduation, believing it was the logical next step. They were bombarded with images of successful marriages through social media and romantic films. The whirlwind romance created a spark of anticipation, painting an optimistic picture of their future. However, as the wedding planning began, the pressure mounted. Friends and family voiced their excitement, yet they also imposed unspoken expectations about how their marriage should unfold.

Emily felt torn between her aspirations and these external pressures. She found herself curating a vision for the perfect wedding: a majestic outdoor ceremony, a lavish reception, and, of course, a picture-perfect couple. Yet, behind the scenes, daily disagreements about trivial matters began to manifest. Jake wanted a smaller affair while Emily felt compelled to live up to the expectations set by their families. The discrepancy between their desires highlighted the first cracks in their relationship.

As the wedding day approached, the stress escalated. The couple's initial enthusiasm began to wane, replaced by exhaustion and anxiety. The pursuit of perfection overshadowed their emotional needs, leading to arguments that left both feeling distant. This experience illustrates how societal expectations can stifle individuality and create a sense of obligation, pushing couples to conform to an idealized version of marriage that may not align with their values.

Such narratives are not uncommon. The expectations surrounding marriage can lead to a slew of complicated feelings, including emotional neglect and disconnection. To navigate societal pressures successfully, couples often feel compelled to suppress their authentic selves, sacrificing individuality on the altar of expectations. The very act of preserving appearances can lead to a marriage built on a foundation of falsehoods, with partners unable to express their true feelings or desires.

Consider the struggles of 'The Skeptic,' a character who has grown increasingly wary of the societal norms surrounding marriage. Observing how friends and family blindly embraced expectations, she began to question whether the traditional routes of marriage, with its clear-cut milestones like purchasing a house and having children, were necessary for her happiness. Meanwhile, her peers seemed trapped in relationships that prioritized tradition and stability over compatibility and love. The Skeptic's internal struggle reflects a broader societal discontent, as many individuals find themselves yearning for authenticity in relationships while grappling with the fears of defying convention.

In a world where social media continuously broadcasts curated highlights of one's life, the pressure to conform intensifies. Couples like Emily and Jake are constantly bombarded with images of others' "perfect" relationships, leading to comparisons and a pervasive sense of inadequacy. As a result, instead of celebrating their unique partnership, they find themselves fixated on how their marriage stacks up against societal expectations, often leading to feelings of failure or disappointment. Unfortunately, the belief that their lives should mirror the glossy portrayals of love and marriage can rob couples of the joy that comes from genuine connection.

Moreover, these societal pressures can have long-reaching consequences. The emotional sacrifices made to align with expectations can lead to disillusionment and, ultimately, heartbreak. A marriage steeped in conformity often breeds resentment, leading partners to feel as though their identities have been subsumed by their roles as spouses. This can manifest in myriad ways, such as lack of communication, emotional withdrawal, or even infidelity.

Take the case of Sarah and Tom, a couple who initially embraced the template of the traditional marriage. Their union began with enthusiasm, driven by mutual respect and love. Yet, as the years rolled on, they started to feel the weight of expectations first experienced during their wedding planning. The couples' individual ambitions took a backseat to the societal norms dictating that they should prioritize their roles as parents and caretakers. Sarah, an aspiring writer, found herself sacrificing her goals to keep up with the demands of family life.

The internal clashes between personal aspirations and societal obligations led to communication breakdowns. Sarah felt increasingly alone in her pursuits, leading to feelings of resentment towards Tom, who was following the more traditional path of climbing the corporate ladder. Over time, their conversations shifted from support and encouragement to bickering and blame. The harmony they once shared unraveled as they confronted the harsh reality that their lives had morphed into one dictated by societal norms rather than one reflective of their true selves.

Revelations like these can be jarring when confronting the dissonance between personal aspirations and societal expectations. Individuals may find themselves longing for fulfillment and authenticity; yet the restrictive nature of societal norms often leaves little room for growth and exploration. The stakes of defying these conventions can feel high, with fears of judgment lurking around every corner.

As we examine the consequences of adhering to societal expectations, we invite reflection upon what a successful marriage should entail. Is it the grand displays of love signified by elaborate weddings, or is it instead the quiet assurance that one's partner knows them deeply? Often, individuals must grapple with how they define their worth within the context of societal expectations versus the personal benchmarks they create for themselves. By emphasizing self-discovery and self-acceptance, we can redefine the parameters that govern our marital experiences.

To illustrate a different approach to marriage, we might consider a couple who confronts their societal conditioning head-on. Mia and Alex, both in their early thirties, entered their marriage with a shared commitment to authenticity over societal norm conformity. They chose a simple ceremony surrounded by their closest friends, choosing personal vows reflecting their journey rather than a tradition dictated by family or culture. Their unequivocal focus on each other's emotional needs and their unwavering commitment to open communication allowed their relationship to flourish, rather than be stifled by external expectations.

The couple ensured that individuality was at the forefront of their relationship. They prioritized each other's passions, with Alex attending Mia's poetry readings and Mia supporting Alex's artistic endeavors. They formed a partnership not bound by the conventional expectations of marriage but instead by mutual respect and a desire for growth, crafting their own narrative. This approach to marriage allowed both Mia and Alex to feel seen, valued, and genuinely loved.

Mia and Alex's experience stands in contrast to Emily and Jake's and serves to illustrate the disparity found within the marriage spectrum. As their relationship blossomed, they became aware that their marriage could serve as a sanctuary from the world's expectations, providing a space where both partners could speak their truths without fear of judgment. Their bond strengthened not just through the union they shared but through challenging the underlying societal pressures that had pervaded their lives.

By juxtaposing diverse experiences, we begin to notice distinct patterns emerge in how couples handle societal expectations related to marriage. While some couples seem to dissolve under pressure, others find ways to thrive when they prioritize authenticity over conformity. The contrasting experiences serve as an invitation for readers to reflect on their relationship journeys through a critical lens.

As we digest these narratives, it becomes increasingly important to challenge the societal expectations that can undermine meaningful connections. It becomes vital for individuals to recognize the distinction between what they genuinely desire and what they have been conditioned to believe should bring them happiness. Through introspection and honest dialogue with one another, couples can better navigate the complexities of their relationships, opening the door to deeper connections.

Breaking free from the chains of societal expectations can be daunting; it often requires courage to confront deeply ingrained beliefs about love and commitment. Yet, finding the strength to challenge these norms can lead to a newfound sense of freedom and personal empowerment. Individuals can reclaim their narratives and craft partnerships based on shared values, mutual respect, and a genuine understanding of one another.

To foster this process of introspection, it is valuable to encourage exploration of one's own motivations for marriage. Are they rooted in authentic love and respect, or are they influenced by external pressures? Couples are invited to engage in candid conversations, bringing their fears, hopes, and expectations to light. This empowered communication lays the groundwork for nurturing authentic connections while simultaneously dismantling the societal restraints that so often dictate the course of relationships.

As we conclude this exploration of societal expectations and their consequences, it's essential to recognize that marriage is deeply personal and multifaceted. Rather than allowing cultural norms to dictate the trajectory of their partnerships, couples are encouraged to create their own definitions of success and fulfillment in marriage. By fostering a spirit of openness and vulnerability, they unlock the potential to craft unique paths reflective of their authentic selves—ultimately ushering in a new era of love and partnership unburdened by the weight of conformity.

In examining these narratives, insights emerge not only about the marriages themselves but also about the societal structures that inform them. The characters' struggles and triumphs collectively form a collective narrative that challenges readers to contemplate how societal expectations have molded their own perceptions of marriage. By engaging with the stories presented, individuals will find inspiration to navigate their relationship journeys with intention and awareness, cultivating authenticity amid a sea of societal pressures. In doing so, they may ultimately discover that love—deep, profound, and genuine—truly flourishes when it is nurtured free from the confines of expectation.

Breaking Down the Myths

Marriage has often been romanticized as a sacred and unbreakable bond, populated with visions of eternal love that flourishes regardless of life's challenges. However, numerous myths surround the institution of marriage, clouding our perceptions and expectations. These myths can insidiously influence our beliefs and decisions, often leading us down paths of disappointment and disillusionment. In this subchapter, we will delve into some of the prevalent myths about marriage, exploring their origins and examining how they contribute to unrealistic expectations.

One of the most pervasive myths is "love conquers all." This age-old belief suggests that genuine love can overcome any barrier; whether its financial troubles, misunderstandings, or even incompatibilities, love is often viewed as the ultimate solution. This myth frequently overlooks the complexities of relationships, including the necessity for mutual effort, communication, and compromise. Love, while undoubtedly a crucial component of a successful partnership, is not a panacea. In reality, the notion that simply loving someone is enough can lead to complacency and an underestimation of the work that relationships entail.

In interviews with relationship therapists, many express frustration over this myth, noting the disservice it does to couples who struggle with the realities of their relationships. Dr. Emily Jamison, a well-regarded marriage counselor, states, "Many couples come to me believing that if they just love each other enough, everything will fall into place. But love is just the starting point; it requires nurturing and active participation from both partners." This perspective highlights how romance can sometimes obscure the necessity for hard work and sacrifice in a relationship.

Consider the story of Marie and James, a couple of

nearly a decade. They began their relationship with an intense passion that convinced them they could conquer anything together. As the years passed, they faced various external challenges, including job losses, familial pressures, and personal crises. Rather than addressing these issues collaboratively, they allowed the weight of their problems to fracture their connection. Marie often reflected on their early days, yearning for the straightforward love that seemed to promise solutions. "I thought love would fix things," she recalls. "But it became clear that it isn't enough when life throws you curveballs."

This myth also leads many to ignore fundamental incompatibilities, convincing themselves that love alone is sufficient to bridge the gaps between them. In truth, while love can foster resilience, it cannot replace essential aspects like compatibility, shared values, and sound communication. Angela, a therapist specializing in couples' counseling, emphasizes this, noting, "Love is powerful, but it's not magic. It doesn't change fundamental differences or resolve conflicts on its own."

A second myth worth examining is the belief that marriage is a cure-all for personal issues. Many enter marriages with the hope that their partner will help to mend their emotional wounds, fulfill unmet needs, or complete their lives. This misconception not only places undue pressure on partners but also perpetuates a cycle of dependency that can stifle individual growth.

Experts warn that viewing marriage as a remedy for personal deficiencies can hinder both partners' development, leading to co-dependent dynamics where one person relies heavily on the other for emotional validation. Dr. Alex Rourke, a clinical psychologist, cautions that "seeking solace in a partner isn't inherently bad, but it can become problematic when it overshadows personal responsibility for your own emotional well-being." This dynamic can breed resentment and dissatisfaction, as the expectation for one person to fulfill multiple roles often proves unrealistic.

Take the story of Samantha, who believed that marrying her high school sweetheart would resolve her struggles with self-worth. She thought that if she could bind her identity with someone else, she would finally feel whole. Yet, as the years progressed, Samantha found herself feeling increasingly lost. "I relied on him to make me happy, and when he couldn't, it felt like our marriage was failing," she reflects. This experience resonated with many who had similarly looked to marriage as a form of emotional salvation.

Recognizing these myths invites us to interrogate our personal beliefs about marriage. How have our experiences, upbringing, and social narratives shaped our understanding? Societal influences—ranging from films and literature to family stories—largely dictate how we form our expectations. Many children grow up consuming fairy tales where love conquers all and ends in a fairy-tale wedding, failing to see the intricacies involved in sustaining a long-term commitment. These narratives often laud idealized notions of partners, reinforcing the fantasy of "the one" who will solve all of life's problems.

To challenge these ingrained myths, we must first take the time to explore our motivations for marriage. Reflective questions can serve as tools for deeper understanding. Ask yourself: What do I believe marriage should provide? Am I entering this union driven by love, societal pressure, or a desire for security? How might these beliefs shape my expectations of my partner and our relationship?

The discomfort can be profound, yet necessary for growth. As couples engage with these questions, they can begin to dismantle the myths that have guided their understanding of marriage, allowing space for more realistic and fulfilling relationships. For instance, couples might realize that while they love each other immensely, they need to actively work on their communication styles and address hurtful patterns in order to cultivate a thriving bond.

As you navigate these reflections, consider conducting an exercise shared by family therapist Laura Mitten, designed to encourage dialogue. Couples can sit down together and discuss five marriage myths that resonate with them. For example, one partner might bring up the notion that "financial stability is a guarantee of happiness" while the other may consider "shared household duties equate to partnership." This creates an opportunity for openness and vulnerability, allowing partners to reassess their beliefs collectively, leading towards a healthier understanding of their marriage.

Moving beyond dismantling myths, this journey compels couples to recognize and emphasize their unique circumstances. Every relationship is distinct, composed of its own dynamics and challenges. Rather than adhering to a blueprint dictated by societal narratives, couples must embrace the individuality of their connection. This can mean establishing clear and concise communication strategies or exploring mutual interests that reflect their shared values and aspirations.

As we scrutinize the myths surrounding marriage, it is essential to consider how they affect our emotional health and relationship dynamics. Professors specializing in psychology reveal the connection between unrealistic expectations and personal dissatisfaction. According to Dr. Helen Frazier, "When couples walk into marriage with the belief that their union will eradicate personal issues, they set themselves up for disappointment. These disillusionments can lead to resentment, unhealthy behaviors, and in some cases, early divorce."

Reflecting on the impact of these myths plays an essential role in fostering accountability. Understanding that no one person can or should fully meet all your emotional needs is the first step towards cultivating healthier relationships. As this awareness develops, individuals become empowered to seek clarity in their emotional experiences, allowing them to express their requirements in ways that can lead to productive discussions with their partners.

To internalize this message, consider the powerful story of Lucas and Michelle. After several years of marriage, they found themselves ensnared in cycles of conflict, particularly regarding finances. Lucas held onto the belief that if their income was sufficient, marital strife would disappear. However, Michelle revealed feelings of inadequacy and stress stemming from their financial discussions. Realizing that their struggles were interlinked, they began redefining their perspectives. They engaged with their feelings, unpacking both their financial duties and emotional expectations.

Through expert consultations and meaningful conversations, they slowly conceded that love alone couldn't fix their challenges. Instead, it became essential for them to create a partnership built on mutual respect, collaboration, and understanding of each other's triggers. They focused on communication, working together to find balance in both personal finance and emotional well-being.

As we reflect upon the myths that influence marriage, it's helpful to consider how open discussions foster empowerment and connection. Addressing misconceptions through dialogue helps build trust, and supports vulnerability, ultimately leading to stronger relationships.

It's crucial to acknowledge that myths around marriage are not purely fabricated; they derive from collective narratives that have been passed down through generations. They may possess some truth, but a rigid adherence to them stunts growth and understanding. Rather than sitting passively within these frameworks, couples should challenge these stories and reshape the narrative that dictates what a marriage should look like and what it entails.

Navigating the labyrinth of myths around marriage demands continuous effort, reflection, and an openness to change. Couples who engage with the realities of their relationships, as opposed to the myths, stand a better chance of fostering authentic love and connection. It's not simply about overcoming false beliefs but seeking to define dependency, emotional health, and partnership on one's own terms.

In moving forward, we encourage a commitment to dispelling myths, promoting insights that resonate with authenticity. With a refined understanding of love and relational dynamics, you can carve your own unique path, leaving behind the oppressive shadows cast by myth. Asking tough questions, embracing personal growth, and committing to mutual support forms the pathway that can lead to genuine connection, away from the deceptive allure of the marriage mirage.

Love vs. Convenience

The Spectrum of Marriage Motivations

Marriage has often been romanticized as the ultimate expression of love, a lifelong commitment born from deep affection and passion. However, a closer examination of modern relationships reveals a more complex reality: many marriages are formed on a spectrum that stretches between genuine love and practical convenience. Understanding this spectrum is key to navigating the often murky waters of modern relationships, where emotional nuances play a significant role in the motivations behind the decision to marry.

At one end of the spectrum lies authentic love—a profound connection characterized by mutual respect, shared goals, and emotional intimacy. This type of love is often accompanied by a desire for partnership and a commitment to grow together. Couples who marry out of genuine affection often describe their relationships as fulfilling and secure, built on a foundation of trust and understanding. Their motivations are rooted in deep emotional bonds that elevate their union beyond mere companionship.

Take, for example, Sarah and James, a couple who met in college. They quickly recognized a unique connection and encouraged each other's dreams. Sarah aspired to be a writer, while James pursued a career in environmental science. Their love was marked by late-night conversations, shared laughter, and a commitment to support one another's ambitions. They were not just partners in romance; they were allies in life. When they married, it was a natural extension of their relationship. Their motivations stemmed from a desire to build a life together, combining their strengths to support shared goals.

However, as we move along the spectrum, we encounter various motivations that are less rooted in authentic love. One significant step down from genuine affection is what might be described as "emotional security." Marriages motivated by emotional security often arise from a desire to mitigate personal fears and insecurities about being alone, both physically and emotionally. Couples in these scenarios may feel pressure from societal expectations or find themselves at a stage in life where settling down appears to be the sensible choice.

Consider the case of Tom and Lisa, both in their late thirties and members of a close-knit community where marriage is seen as a rite of passage. Both had experienced heartbreak in past relationships and began to feel the societal pressure to conform to expected norms. While they appreciated one another and sought companionship, their motivations leaned toward finding security rather than a deep emotional connection. Marrying for emotional security led them to overlook critical aspects of their relationship, which ultimately exposed underlying tensions they hadn't fully addressed.

Next on the spectrum is practical convenience. Marriages formed from a desire for practical arrangements can arise from various scenarios, including financial stability, shared living situations, or social status. In these partnerships, love may not be the driving force; instead, logistical concerns often take precedence. Couples may justify their decision to marry through rationalization, convincing themselves that practicality will yield lasting happiness.

A vivid illustration of this motivation can be found in the story of Rachel and Steve. Both professionals in fast-paced careers, they decided to marry primarily for convenience. They shared an apartment, splitting the rent and household responsibilities, and believed that being married would simplify their lives. Their relationship was functional but lacked the emotional depth that many associate with marriage. In this case, the convenience of their arrangement overshadowed the genuine desire for love, leading to feelings of loneliness even while living under the same roof.

As we progress further down the spectrum, we come to what many consider opportunistic attachments. Marriages based on opportunistic motives are often rocky, rooted in a desire to gain something—be it social status, financial benefits, or a sense of security. These unions can be problematic due to the underlying motivations that ultimately dilute the potential for genuine affection.

Take, for example, the story of William and Jessica. William, a successful entrepreneur, was pursued by many but ultimately married Jessica, a woman who appeared to press all the right buttons for his public image. Jessica was ambitious and socially savvy, and their union provided both of them with benefits in terms of reputation and social standing. However, the marriage was little more than a strategic alliance. Their relationship lacked emotional intimacy, as both focused on the advantages the marriage brought rather than building a genuine bond.

The emotional nuances that motivate marriages are not static; they can evolve over time. Couples may begin their journey with practical convenience, only to develop deeper feelings for one another as they create shared experiences and navigate life's challenges together. Conversely, a marriage built on genuine affection can deteriorate into a partnership defined by convenience if not nurtured beyond the initial spark.

The Advocate reminds readers that recognizing one's motivation is critical. Understanding where one falls on the spectrum can lead to better decisions about relationships. Questions like "What do I truly want from this partnership?" and "Am I genuinely connecting with my partner, or are we simply coexisting?" are essential to self-reflection. Couples may find themselves grappling with this internal dialogue as they consider whether they should continue to pursue their relationship or if they'd be better off apart.

This introspective journey is illustrated through the narratives of characters who find themselves at various points on the spectrum. For many, the challenge is in reconciling their motivations with their current reality. The tension between love and convenience often manifests in moments of doubt, where couples are compelled to evaluate the authenticity of their connection. The emotional weight of these reflections can be significant, as individuals wrestle with feelings of disappointment, longing, or the fear of failure.

Consider the story of a couple, Maria and David, who started as best friends before realizing their feelings for each other. They believed they'd found authentic love, yet over the years, the practicality of their lives became a dominant force in their relationship. As their careers evolved and life responsibilities piled up, the vibrant connection they once shared waned. They often found themselves functioning like a business partnership—managing bills, chores, and children—rather than nurturing the love that once sparked their marriage. This shift in focus led to emotional disconnection and dissatisfaction.

In her journey, Maria faced a turning point that required her to confront the motivations that led her down the aisle. She asked herself difficult questions: "Am I staying because I love David, or have I become complacent in our arrangement?" Her struggle to reconnect with her feelings mirrored many others journeying through the marriage spectrum. This internal reflection became a catalyst for change, enabling Maria to reconnect with the essence of their bond, initiating a vital dialogue that reignited their connection.

Marriages that begin with opportunistic attachments can often lead to heartbreak when the initial benefits wane. Partners who pursue marriage out of convenience without emotional connections often find themselves at a crossroads when ambitions shift or circumstances change. The case of Claire and Mark, who married in their twenties after a whirlwind romance, highlights the pitfalls of such motivations. After years of navigating career changes and family dynamics, they realized that the foundational motivations for their marriage—financial stability and societal pressure—had overshadowed any remnants of love. With the connection that once sparked their union fading, they faced the difficult decision of whether to end their marriage or work toward rekindling their bond.

Through scenarios like these, The Advocate offers a guiding framework for readers to assess their motivations. Encouragement to explore deeper emotional undercurrents becomes a vital exploration of self-awareness. Engaging reflective prompts, such as "What core motivations brought me to this relationship?" or "How have our motivations shifted over time?" help individuals dissect the layers of their partnerships to recognize authentic connections that may be buried beneath those rooted in convenience.

The spectrum of marriage motivations shines a light on the reality that love can be complex, evolving based on personal circumstances, societal expectations, and individual desires. Recognizing where one fits on that spectrum can offer insights and guidance for navigating challenges in one's relationship.

In conclusion, understanding the spectrum of marriage motivations empowers individuals to reflect on their journeys thoughtfully. By examining where their motivations lie—whether in the realm of genuine love, emotional security, practical convenience, or opportunistic attachments—couples can gain clarity and insight into their personal narratives. As they traverse the ups and downs of relationships, maintaining awareness of their motivations allows them to consciously choose paths that lead to deeper emotional connections and authentic partnerships. The journey toward understanding one's motivations is essential for cultivating love that goes beyond convenience, ultimately ensuring that marriage remains a profound and meaningful journey rather than a mere transactional arrangement.

The Cost of Convenience

In the tapestry of modern relationships, the decision to marry for convenience rather than love has become an all-too-common narrative. For many, the allure of practicality—having a partner who contributes to finances, providing a semblance of stability, or fulfilling societal expectations—can overshadow the more intangible, yet vital, components of a healthy relationship like emotional connection, intimacy, and genuine partnership. As we delve into this phenomenon, we will explore the emotional ramifications of these seemingly pragmatic choices, illustrated through real-life stories that illuminate the unseen costs of convenience in marriage.

Consider the story of Sarah and Jake, two young professionals who met during their college years. At first glance, their relationship appeared nearly picture-perfect—both ambitious, financially secure, and eager to settle down. At the age of 30, they decided to marry, citing the desire to own a home together and build their careers as the driving forces behind their commitment. To Sarah, the idea of living with Jake in their own house, enjoying the stability it brought, seemed like an opportunity too good to pass up. And Jake appreciated Sarah's practicality and shared goals.

However, as the months rolled into years, the initial excitement faded into a disheartening routine. Their conversations shifted from dreams and ambitions to household chores and financial planning. Both individuals assumed, naively, that being good partners meant fulfilling expectations rather than nurturing their feelings for one another. It wasn't long before the emotional disconnection began to manifest. What had once felt like an exciting partnership became a mundane existence—a series of transactional interactions. Despite sharing space and responsibilities, they often found themselves in silent, contemplative solitude rather than engaging in heartfelt discussions. The emotional connection they had in college, once filled with passion and spark, dissipated into an echo of obligation.

Sarah often wrapped herself in layers of anger and resentment as she reflected on her feelings. The excitement of their wedding day had morphed into an endless cycle of bills, responsibilities, and unsaid words. Jake, too, felt the weight of their convenience-driven marriage but didn't realize until it was too late that he had voided the deeper connection they once shared. Instead of exploring each other's emotional landscapes, they avoided difficult conversations, creating an emotional chasm that resembled an insurmountable wall built from their everyday decisions.

This tale of Sarah and Jake is one repeated in various forms across countless marriages. Many couples choose partners based on factors like shared financial stability, social prestige, or familial approval, often citing these as rational reasons for their decisions. However, what tends to happen is an eventual realization that while they may have checked boxes on a practical list, they neglected to carve out space for the deeply intertwined emotions that foster true partnership. The cost of this convenience becomes a slow-burning resentment that disrupts the harmony in their lives together.

Reflecting beyond Sarah and Jake, consider the perspective of Tom and Lisa. Their relationship exemplified the classic trope of marrying for convenience; they both met in a time of life when their career trajectories aligned, and their choices were woven together out of shared financial goals. For Lisa, Tom represented stability; for Tom, Lisa was the perfect partner to raise a family. Their union seemed sensible and efficient on paper, a perfect pairing that merited marriage. Yet, beneath the surface, both Lisa and Tom wrestled with unaddressed dreams and ambitions.

As Lisa immersed herself in the daily routines of motherhood, she gradually became aware of her unfulfilled desires for independence and career progression. Child-rearing consumed her identity, and she lost sight of who she was before becoming "Tom's wife" or "the kids' mother." Tom, on the other hand, increasingly felt overwhelmed with the pressures of being a sole provider. He thought marrying Lisa meant he would not have to worry. Instead, he found himself resenting his own choices. Every late-night work email and missed family dinner festered into bitterness, amplifying the void that had invaded their relationship.

The growing distances between them ultimately led to misunderstandings and constant blame. Lisa felt trapped, longing to reclaim a sense of individuality and purpose beyond her parental role, while Tom felt increasingly burdened by the expectations and pressures of supporting his family alone. The concept of convenience that had brought them together became a source of pain that drove them apart.

These narratives underscore a crucial lesson: when convenience drives a relationship, emotional disconnection becomes its shadow. Without genuine emotions to bind them, partners often become mere cohabitants, orchestrating lives that function on external validation rather than heartfelt connection. The painstaking toll of prioritizing practical decisions over emotional resonance can lead to a pervasive sense of dissatisfaction, posing difficult questions for reflection.

Why do we marry? It's a question that merits profound introspection. Many individuals find themselves navigating societal expectations or the allure of pragmatic living, propelled by cultural narratives that prioritize stability over intimacy. Too often, the pursuit of convenience clouds our judgment and limits our capacity for genuine connection. Instead of examining the foundations of love, individuals often find themselves swallowed by external pressures, leaving them emotionally starved in a partnership that feels more like a business venture than a romantic journey.

Sarah and Jake's journey continued to unfold under the weight of their choices. As time wore on, they reached an inflection point— a crossroads stemming from the realization that the shared vision they once held had crumbled into a series of hollow agreements. In moments of honesty, they'd share their frustrations, but fear dampened their voices, leading to silent breakfasts and long walks home after work where the companionship felt less like kinship and more like cohabitation. Emotional loneliness thrived in their silence, as if guarded walls urging them to maintain the appearance of harmony yet causing deeper rifts in their bond.

Recognizing the detrimental effects of their choices, both Sarah and Jake sought therapy to traverse the labyrinth of their emotional landscape. In therapy, they discovered the underlying wounds that festered from their decisions—to prioritize money and stability at the cost of their emotional rapport. Each session forced them to peel back layers of defense, confronting raw emotions and hidden desires that had long been stifled beneath their comfortable façade.

After extensive conversations and deep emotional exploration, they began to rekindle the intimacy that had been lost. It took work, understanding, and an unyielding commitment to vulnerability; however, ultimately, they found a new way to navigate their marriage. They learned to revisit shared dreams, cultivate emotional empathy, and allow themselves to express their evolving needs. The burning resentment that once loomed dissipated as they began to forge a deeper bond, one predicated not merely on the appearance of compatibility, but rather on an emotional foundation that allowed them to grow together.

In a similar journey, Tom and Lisa discovered that addressing the cost of convenience required painful vulnerability and openness. They initiated conversations about their individual desires and dreams they've clipped in favor of convenience. Gradually, it became clear that Lisa craved the chance to explore her professional ambitions, while Tom yearned to share parenting responsibilities more equitably. Realigning their understanding of what partnership meant for them, they took proactive steps to create space for communication and compromise within their relationship dynamic.

Lisa sought out professional development opportunities to reignite her passion for her career while ensuring she communicated effectively with Tom about her aspirations. Tom, in turn, made a concerted effort to be more present at home, supporting Lisa in achieving her goals by staggering work commitments. Their willingness to let go of preconceived notions about marriage propelled them into a new, compassionate territory, one in which both partners felt respected and valued as individuals and collaborators.

Ultimately, the journeys of Sarah and Jake and Tom and Lisa reveal the costly fallout of marrying for convenience over authentic love. What initially appeared to be practical choices led to emotional disconnection, neglect, and resentment because the heart of the relationship remained undernourished. Their stories illuminate the profound truth that a relationship built solely on convenience can become a hollow shell, devoid of the warmth and connection necessary for enduring love.

As partners embark on their relationship journeys, it's essential to reflect on long-term implications. Are you prioritizing the pragmatic, convenient aspects of love at the expense of genuine connection? What does your relationship say about your core values and desires? These are crucial questions demanding introspection, spurring readers to critically evaluate their relationship choices.

Ultimately, we must aim to recognize the dangers that lurk within the comfort of convenience-driven commitments—acknowledge that such decisions can yield emotional narratives filled with unfulfilled yearnings, muted desires, and an enduring sense of disenchantment.

Through these poignant stories, readers are called to examine their motivations for choosing partners. While the allure of convenience is captivating, it is vital to apprehend the heavy emotional cost associated with placing practicality above emotional intimacy. Love requires more than the surface-level regard of convenience; it seeks depth, connection, and authenticity to flourish. In building relationships that transcend mere convenience, individuals can create partnerships that inspire growth, fulfillment, and joy, transforming the way we view love and commitment for generations to come.

The Quest for True Love

In a world that often prioritizes convenience over depth, the quest for true love can feel like a daunting journey. From the fairy tales we were told as children to the romantic comedies that fill our screens, the ideal of finding a soulmate is woven into the fabric of our societal narrative. Yet, beneath this glamorous facade lies a complex reality that often leaves individuals longing for a deeper connection. As we embark on this subchapter, we will explore the vital importance of seeking true love—one that transcends superficial attachments—to cultivate lasting partnerships rooted in emotional compatibility and shared values.

True love isn't merely found; it's built. It requires a foundation of honest self-reflection and an understanding of what we truly desire from our relationships. To begin this exploration, let's start with the first step: introspection. Understanding ourselves is paramount to identifying the kind of love we seek. Individuals often enter relationships with preconceived notions, influenced by external narratives and societal expectations. Yet, the most meaningful connections arise when we peel back the layers of external pressure, allowing our authentic selves to emerge.

One primary guideline for introspection is to assess what love means to you personally. Are you drawn to the idea of partnership out of a deep desire for affection, or are you influenced by societal norms telling you that marriage is a prerequisite for happiness? Ask yourself the following questions: What are my core beliefs about love? What qualities do I seek in a partner? What does a fulfilling relationship look like for me? These inquiries can serve as a compass, guiding us toward meaningful connections rather than superficial pairings.

As we navigate our personal quests for love, emotional compatibility emerges as a vital component in establishing a strong bond with our partners. What does emotional compatibility entail? It is the ability to connect on a deeper level, understanding each other's feelings and needs genuinely. When two individuals share similar emotional languages, they can communicate openly, empathize, and support each other through life's trials. This balance is crucial, as emotional disconnection is often at the heart of relationships plagued by strife.

Consider the journey of Sarah and James. Their relationship began with undeniable chemistry—an attraction fueled by passion and physical appeal. Initially, they reveled in each other's company, intoxicatingly intertwined in the haze of newfound love. However, as time progressed, cracks began to show. They discovered their foundational emotional needs were misaligned; Sarah valued security and open communication, while James thrived on independence and occasional solitude. The disparity in their emotional frameworks led to miscommunications and misunderstandings that would eventually culminate in a painful breakup.

In contrast, consider Emily and Marcus, whose connection developed slowly but steadily. Their relationship was grounded in mutual vulnerability and a shared understanding of one another's emotional intricacies. Emily, an introvert who valued quiet time, found resonance with Marcus, who appreciated deep conversations and emotional nurturing. They prioritized shared experiences that fostered intimacy, like weekend hikes that allowed them space to connect without distractions. Unlike Sarah and James, Emily and Marcus invested in each other's emotional worlds, creating a connection that would withstand the inevitable challenges life presented.

As we delve deeper into the importance of seeking true love, the next facet to consider is shared values. Values form the bedrock upon which relationships are built. They inform our decisions, shape our lives, and drive our ambitions. A partnership is bound to flourish when both individuals share similar core values—be it family, career aspirations, spiritual beliefs, or life goals.

To illustrate this point, let's consider the story of Lena and Raj. Lena envisioned a life filled with travel and adventure, her heart set on exploring different cultures and experiencing the world. In contrast, Raj held a more traditional view; his dream was to build a stable life in their hometown, focusing on career growth and establishing a family. Despite their affection for each other, the conflict of desires created an underlying tension that led to frequent disagreements. Over time, each partner felt the weight of sacrifice, as neither could fully honor their passions without resentment.

On the other hand, consider the union of Mia and Adam, who discovered a shared commitment to social justice and community service early in their relationship. This common value not only intensified their bond but also provided a framework for them to collaborate on projects aimed at making a difference. Their relationship thrived as they supported each other's ambitions and celebrated their joint endeavors, guiding them to build a life underscored by purpose and fulfillment.

It's crucial to acknowledge that seeking true love is not merely about finding someone who mirrors our hopes and desires; it's also about navigating the complexities of human nature. Emotional compatibility and shared values foster connections, but every relationship consists of unique challenges, misunderstandings, and moments of vulnerability. Navigating these nuances requires open communication—an essential thread that binds true love.

Practicing effective communication enables partners to tackle the obstacles that arise during their journey together. Sharing feelings, needs, and vulnerabilities fosters an environment of trust and understanding. When love is built on honesty, partners become allies who can face life's adversities together, strengthening their bond in the process.

For instance, let's explore the fictional relationship of Zoe and Max. Initially, they struggled to convey their feelings, often bottling up frustrations to avoid conflict. Zoe, a highly sensitive person, found it challenging to articulate her needs, while Max, who tended to be more stoic, felt overwhelmed by emotional discussions. Their relationship began to deteriorate due to the lack of open dialogue. It wasn't until Zoe initiated a heart-to-heart conversation about her emotional landscape that things began to shift. By dissecting the anxieties that plagued them both, they created a roadmap toward better communication. This effort led to mutual understanding and emotional support, establishing an unbreakable bond that flourished from a foundation of vulnerability.

A significant takeaway from the discussions around true love is the recognition that love should bring more than just comfort; it should elicit growth. As partners, we should inspire each other to evolve, challenging one another to reach higher and achieve our full potential. The pursuit of this kind of love encourages us to foster an environment where both individuals can thrive, leaning into shared aspirations while maintaining a sense of autonomy.

In light of all these considerations, how can we translate the quest for true love into actionable steps? Let's delve into a framework that encourages introspection, enhances emotional compatibility, reinforces shared values, and fosters open communication.

The first step involves self-reflection. Set aside time to journal your thoughts on what you seek in a relationship. Write down your desires, fears, and dreams. This exercise not only clarifies your intentions but also reveals potential obstacles you may thwart in your quest for love. With this newfound awareness, you'll better understand what constitutes a fulfilling relationship for you personally.

Next, seek to engage in open discussions with your

partner regarding emotional needs and aspirations. Establish a routine—perhaps a weekly check-in—where you can delve into deeper conversations about your emotions, dreams, and the directions in which you want your relationship to grow. This practice can pave the way for empathy and provide insights into each other's inner worlds.

In parallel, make it a priority to examine the values that matter to you. Create a shared values map with your partner. Discuss your individual values and brainstorming how they can coexist and what common ground can be achieved to build a unified vision for your relationship. This exercise deepens the connection and presents opportunities for alignment in your goals.

Additionally, foster the habit of supporting each other's personal growth. Encourage your partner to pursue their passions and take risks, whether big or small. Celebrate achievements, big and small, reinforcing the belief that love is a partnership that thrives through individual fulfillment.

Finally, never underestimate the power of constructive communication. Whenever conflicts arise, commit to addressing them openly and constructively. Approach discussions with empathy, expressing your feelings, listening actively, and seeking collaborative resolutions. Remember, the goal isn't to "win" the argument but to strengthen your bond through understanding. As we approach the culmination of this subchapter, it's crucial to reiterate the urgency of prioritizing true love over fleeting attachments. Superficial relationships are often built on convenience, leading to discontent and heartache. By consciously opting for emotional compatibility, shared values, and open communication, we create an environment conducive to genuine connection.

The quest for true love may not always be a straight path; it is often fraught with challenges and unexpected turns. But by embracing introspection and authenticity, we equip ourselves with the tools needed to foster meaningful relationships. These very relationships are what will ultimately enrich our lives—nurturing our souls and providing a deep sense of connection that transcends the superficial.

As you embark on your journey of love, remember to prioritize the deeper connections that illuminate your essence. True love is not merely an end goal but a journey of exploration, growth, and shared experiences. It invites you to reflect on your values, nurture your emotional landscape, and communicate honestly with your partner. Embrace the quest for true love, and you just may find that the most profound connections await in spaces of authenticity, vulnerability, and genuine affection. As you dive into the complexities of love, may you discover the beauty of true companionship—one that endures through the challenges and triumphs alike. The journey awaits.

The Statistics Speak

Data-Driven Insights

In recent years, numerous studies have scrutinized the motivations behind marriage, bringing to light various statistics that paint a complex picture of modern relationships. These statistics reveal that many individuals enter marriage for reasons that are often surprisingly divorced from the romantic ideals we hear about in popular culture. The findings highlight a prevalence for non-romantic motivations, such as financial security, societal pressure, and familial expectations, which can lay the groundwork for future discontent and emotional turmoil.

According to a comprehensive survey conducted by the American Psychological Association, approximately 60% of respondents indicated that financial stability was a significant motivation in their decision to marry. This statistic is particularly striking when one considers that financial health is a core component of overall well-being. Marriages often begin with discussions about shared financial goals, debt management, and the security of combined resources. While these discussions are pragmatic and essential for a healthy partnership, they can overshadow the more sentimental aspects of love and devotion. The implication here is that when economic factors take precedence over emotional compatibility, couples are at risk of entering a contract that prioritizes monetary gain over mutual affection.

Furthermore, data from the Pew Research Center illustrates how societal norms shape the decision to marry.

A staggering 70% of respondents noted feeling pressure from family or societal expectations to tie the knot. These pressures can stem from cultural narratives about the age at which one should marry, the perceived necessity of marriage in establishing family units, and the expectation to conform to historical precedents. This societal pressure can create a fertile ground for marriages that are entered into without full consideration of personal desire or emotional connection. Here, we find that the weight of societal expectation can lead individuals down a path where the marriage itself might feel like an obligation rather than a choice grounded in love.

'The Researcher' provides insights into how these motivations can engender feelings of inadequacy and resentment. The statistics suggest that when emotional needs are unmet due to misplaced priorities, couples may experience a decline in relational satisfaction over time. The American Institute of Marriage highlights that nearly 50% of marital conflicts stem from financial disagreements—indicating a clear link between those pragmatic motivations for marriage and later discontent within relationships. The Researcher attributes this to a disconnect between expectations and reality; when financial security takes precedence over genuine love, couples may find their unions fraught with tension.

Several personal narratives highlight the trends suggested by these statistics. For example, consider the story of Sarah and Tom, a couple who married in their late twenties after a whirlwind romance during college. Initial attraction was built on emotional intimacy, but as they moved into their first apartment together and started merging finances, the excitement waned. They found themselves arguing about money constantly, exacerbated by student loans and contrasting spending habits. Tom was focused on saving for a house, while Sarah preferred to enjoy their young years by traveling and exploring. Despite love being the initial motivating factor in their relationship, the intrusion of pragmatic concerns drove a wedge between them, showcasing a real-life scenario in which financial stability overshadowed genuine affection.

Moreover, the "Marital Happiness" report published by the National Institute of Family Studies reveals that couples who report marrying for love versus convenience are significantly happier in their relationships after five years. The data indicates that upwards of 75% of those who entered marriage primarily out of love considered their unions to be fulfilling compared to only 45% of those who cited convenience as their main motivation. These findings underscore the profound emotional ramifications of entering a marriage based on non-romantic factors, highlighting an alarming trend that permeates modern marriage.

The perspective of 'The Advocate' further complicates this landscape. They often emphasize the importance of acknowledging these motivations before entering into lifelong commitments. Acknowledging a partner's motivations, whether they align with romantic ideals or not, can be crucial in developing an understanding of what drives individual decisions. 'The Advocate' has encountered couples whose conversations about financial stability dominate relationship discussions, and they recommend not merely acknowledging these pragmatic considerations but fostering open dialogue about each partner's emotional needs.

In another poignant illustration, we turn to Jenna and Mark, who married in their early thirties amid societal expectations rooted in their upbringing. Both were the elder siblings in families that valued marriage as a rite of passage, and they felt compelled to follow suit. While they respected each other and shared many interests, Jenna often felt only a half-hearted connection to the idea of marriage, believing it more of an obligation than a choice. The pressure from their families created a sense of urgency that rushed their engagement, yet once married, both struggled with the reality of their decision. Despite achieving financial discussions about their shared future, their emotional connection remained superficial, and over time, they faced significant challenges in navigating this disconnect.

Adding to these complexities is the notion of the "financial marriage," a term that has emerged in discussions around modern relationships. Research by the Institute for Marriage and Public Policy indicates that around 40% of couples marry primarily for financial reasons, including benefitting from tax structures, dual incomes, and combined healthcare plans. This functionally economic view on marriage points to a rearrangement of traditional motivations initially rooted in romance for many millennials and younger couples. The idea that marriage can serve as a financial contract underscores the transformation of personal relationships and begs the question of whether genuine intimacy is losing ground to practicality.

Another recent survey conducted by the National Marriage Project offered some alarming insights; around 50% of participants believed that marriage is simply a tax arrangement. While not all participants expressed such stark views, this perspective highlights a critical shift in the way younger generations view marriage. Many of those surveyed expressed feelings of cynicism regarding the permanence of marriage, viewing it through the lens of financial optimization rather than emotional fulfillment. This change signals a broader cultural shift where love may take a backseat to pragmatism transforming marriage from a symbol of love into a vehicle for financial convenience or societal acceptability.

The tapestry of these statistics is illustrative of a narrative promoted by 'The Researcher,' who continues to harvest insights from the growing body of literature surrounding relationship dynamics. Their assessments indicate that the undeniable statistics surrounding financial security, family pressure, and societal expectations influence individuals in complex ways, driving them to make life-altering decisions without properly taking stock of their own emotional well-being.

In a contrasting relationship example, we meet Lucy and Adam, who embarked on their marriage with an unwavering belief tested by public expectations. Before becoming engaged, they spent significant time discussing the nature of their relationship, weighing their mutual love against the backdrop of their respective financial situations. Unlike many of their peers, they made a conscious choice to prioritize emotional compatibility before agreeing to marry. This decision led to the establishment of clear boundaries and open communication, fostering a strong emotional connection that would serve them well through any financial challenge that arose. Their story serves as a beacon of hope, advocating for authentic relationship foundations based on mutual affection rather than external pressures.

As these narratives converge, it becomes increasingly clear that understanding the motivations that drive marriages is crucial for future success. The myriad statistics, expert commentary, and personal stories illustrate a considerable need for introspection when considering marriage. By fostering awareness and addressing the underlying motivations behind unions, couples can create the environment necessary for flourishing relationships marked by partnership and love.

It is essential for individuals entering into marriage to reflect on their motivations genuinely. Recognizing whether one is motivated by love, lust, financial factors, or social expectations can enrich the experience of partnership. As evidenced by the growing literature on marital satisfaction, emotional connection, and open communication yield a transformative impact on relationships. The findings presented here provide an opportunity for individuals to engage in self-discovery and pursuit of clarity about their desires and needs.

In sums, the data collected and analyzed by 'The Researcher' not only uncovers the various motivations behind marriage but also serves as a critical tool for individuals seeking deeper understanding of their relationships. As society continues to evolve, it is essential that we remain attuned to the underlying factors that shape our unions, embracing the complexities of love, commitment, and expectation—a journey that, when approached with mindfulness and clarity, offers the promise of sustainable joy and connection. This ongoing dialogue informs our understanding of relationships, guiding us toward more authentic partnerships founded upon shared values and genuine love rather than mere convenience or societal expectancy. The juxtaposition of statistical analysis with personal narratives highlights the nuances of marriage in a modern context, underscoring the importance of cultivating emotional awareness amid prevailing societal pressures and financial considerations.

Ultimately, the conversation surrounding marriage must evolve as we uncover these truths, providing a pathway towards healthier, more fulfilling connections in our relationships. As we navigate these complex waters, we must embrace the call for authenticity, encouraging bold and thoughtful exploration of our motivations, desires, and connections with one another. The statistics do not only reveal trends; they invite us to engage, reflect, and ultimately redefine what love and partnership can and should mean in our lives.

Dissecting the Numbers

As we delve deeper into the intricate tapestry of marriage motivations, it's essential to transition from the bare statistics and their stark implications to a more nuanced interpretation of what these numbers truly signify. The statistics presented previously provide a foundation for understanding the shifting landscape of romantic partnerships, but understanding the "why" behind these numbers is equally crucial. This subchapter aims to dissect the underlying psychological and social factors that contribute to the motivations behind marriage and to explore the generational shifts that have influenced how individuals perceive love and commitment today.

Consider the statistic that roughly 80% of partnerships contain at least one individual whose motivations for marriage diverge from the ideals of genuine love and commitment. At first glance, it's an alarming figure, hinting at a pervasive discontent that could undermine the very fabric of marital unions. However, as we dig into this statistic, we find that these numbers reflect not merely individual desires but broader social and cultural influences that shape our understanding of relationships.

The traditional narrative of marriage has evolved significantly over the decades. Historically, marriage was often a calculated arrangement based on economic necessity, social status, or familial obligation. Love, as a primary motivation for marriage, was rarely at the forefront. In today's context, this shift is multifaceted. Economic independence, particularly among women, has allowed for a greater emphasis on personal choice in selecting a partner. Yet, this independence has also introduced complications, as many individuals grapple with the contrasting expectations of romantic love versus practical necessity.

Let us consider the experiences of two fictional characters, Emily and Jake, who epitomize different approaches to marriage in today's world. Emily, in her early thirties, grew up in a household that championed romantic love. Her parents, though divorced, often spoke of the passion and connection they once shared. For Emily, the idea of marrying for anything less than love seemed not only undesirable but also irresponsible. Conversely, Jake, also in his thirties, comes from a background where practical considerations were paramount. His parents encouraged him to seek a partner who could contribute to a stable lifestyle, irrespective of whether or not love was the primary factor.

When Emily and Jake meet, their differing motivations for marriage become a focal point of their budding relationship. Emily's insistence on emotional connection leads her to resist the notion of pragmatic arrangements, while Jake's upbringing makes him more accepting of a partnership that balances both love and practicality. As they navigate their relationship, Emily finds herself contemplating societal expectations as she grapples with her desire for love against Jake's sincere wish for stability, which he views as a foundation for love to flourish.

In dissecting their motivations, we see how generational differences play out. Emily embodies a generation that embraces the idea of love-centric marriage, fueled by the media's romanticized portrayal of relationships. She is influenced by the narratives of love stories that dominate popular culture—think of cinematic romances where love conquers all obstacles. On the other hand, Jake's perspective stems from a generation that witnessed economic downturns and shifting job markets, which emphasized the need for security, shared financial goals, and partnership over pure sentimentality. The precariousness of modern life has led him to view marriage through a practical lens, valuing cooperation over romance.

This interplay between tradition and modernity is a key component of what drives the numbers we see reflected in modern marriage statistics. The increasing acceptance of cohabitation, the rise in age at first marriage, and the growing willingness to leave unsatisfactory relationships all point to a shift in societal norms surrounding commitment. Additionally, the emergence of same-sex marriage has added layers of complexity, expanding the definition of partnership and drawing attention to the diverse motivations that inform individual choices.

As we embrace these generational shifts, we should also acknowledge the psychological factors at play. The desire for validation, security, and belonging often emerges in discussions of relationship motivations. Individuals are wired to seek connection, yet the methods through which they pursue that connection can vary markedly based on their past experiences and psychological needs.

Reflect on the stories of multiple individuals across different demographics who have shared their marriage experiences. Take, for example, Sarah, an African American woman in her late twenties whose life has been shaped by the challenges faced by her community. Growing up witnessing a lack of stable marriages in her neighborhood, Sarah feels a powerful urge to create a family grounded in love and fidelity, not just for her own satisfaction but as a cultural statement that defies historical trends in her community. Her motivation is rooted in both psychological needs—such as the desire for stability—and social factors, like empowerment through family building.

In contrast, we can look at Marcus, a Latino man in his early forties. His experiences differ markedly from Sarah's, as he has enjoyed a family background that values marriage as a cultural cornerstone. For him, marrying a partner who shares similar values and traditions becomes more than a personal desire; it's a way to honor his lineage and maintain cultural continuity. This act of marriage becomes a sacred bond not just between him and his partner but also between families, reinforcing social ties that transcend individual desires.

Marcus's views on marriage reflect broader societal expectations that vary across cultures and generations. While he sees marriage as an essential part of life, Sarah's approach is more about redefining norms and breaking cycles. This divergence encapsulates the complexity of motivations that shape romantic partnerships today, bridging personal desires with the weight of societal expectations.

The internal reflections of these characters allow us to explore their decisions more deeply. Sarah finds herself contemplating the pressures she feels as a woman who desires love, stability, and autonomy. This internal conflict exposes her to the challenges of navigating societal expectations while forging her path. Meanwhile, Marcus, having experienced the communal expectations of marriage, wrestles with feeling somewhat bound by tradition yet eager to embrace modernity in his partnership.

Reflecting on these complexities enriches our understanding of the statistics at hand. By encouraging readers to view numbers through a lens of personal stories, we humanize the data and reveal the emotional landscapes that inform decisions about marriage. The disparities between the motivations of Sarah, Marcus, Emily, and Jake demonstrate that there is no one-size-fits-all narrative when it comes to love and commitment. Instead, the motivations for marriage resonate on a spectrum, shaped by individual experiences, cultural backgrounds, and psychological needs.

As we dive deeper into generational differences, it's also essential to explore how past relationships inform present desires. For many, the specter of previous unions—whether they are personal divorces, the unions of parents, or even friendships that soured—casts a long shadow over the decision to marry. Understanding this influence can illuminate why certain individuals gravitate towards pragmatic arrangements while others cling fervently to the idealized notions of true love.

Let's turn to another character, Lisa, a woman in her mid-thirties who has gone through a tumultuous relationship in her past. After enduring heart-wrenching betrayals and emotional struggles, she is left questioning whether love is worth the pain it often brings. In her journey toward healing, Lisa becomes involved in a relationship with Mark, a man who embodies kindness, stability, and understanding. Despite Mark's deep affection for her, Lisa frequently falters in fully committing because her experiences have instilled a deep-seated fear of vulnerability. The numbers tell us about the percentage of individuals who marry out of convenience—but Lisa's story illustrates that the reasons behind these decisions are often interwoven with personal trauma and unresolved emotional struggles.

Mark, understanding this complexity, endeavors to help Lisa navigate her fears. He embodies a sense of patience and encourages open conversations. Their interactions reveal Lisa's internal dialogue—questions about whether she can let her guard down and embrace vulnerability for the sake of love. The emotional weight of her past creates a pathway toward understanding, shedding light on how individuals may choose partnership for security rather than romantic ideals.

When exploring the implications of statistics on marriage motivations, it becomes evident that these narratives can forge a sense of connection among readers. Individuals who recognize their struggles mirrored in characters like Lisa, Sarah, or Marcus may find solace in understanding that they are not alone in navigating conflicting motivations.

The impact of awareness surrounding these statistics is profound. As readers reflect on their own motivations through the stories shared, they are invited to scrutinize their perspectives on love and commitment. In doing so, they may wish to step away from societal pressures or romanticized ideals that have previously clouded their judgment. By confronting the inner workings of their hearts and minds, readers can empower themselves to make informed decisions rooted in authenticity rather than convenience.

Furthermore, as we analyze generational differences, we must acknowledge that societal expectations are not static. They shift and morph in response to economic realities, evolving cultural norms, and the collective experiences of individuals. The statistics reveal a reality that is fluid, a dance between the past and the present. This interconnectedness of personal experiences and broader societal changes empowers individuals to question the motivations driving their choices and to lean into conversations about love that prioritize authenticity and emotional understanding.

As we conclude this exploration of the statistics

surrounding marriage motivations, it's crucial to emphasize that the tapestry of human experience is rich and layered—filled with stories of hope, struggle, and eventual resilience. Whether one frames their journey through the lens of love, practicality, or a blend of both, the key lies in open dialogue, introspection, and a willingness to embrace the nuanced landscapes of relationships.

In stripping away the numbing statistics and engaging with the real-life implications behind them, we are granted insights that are transformative. The data is not merely numbers; it represents the sentiments, scars, aspirations, and healing journeys of those navigating the labyrinth of marriage today. Understanding this can lead not just too personal reflection but also to fostering a more compassionate understanding of love in all its complexity. Embracing these varying motivations not only enhances the relationships we build but also allows us to navigate the intricate world of commitment with greater empathy and awareness.

The Impact of Awareness

Understanding the statistics surrounding marriage can serve as a crucial turning point in how individuals and couples navigate their relationships. While numbers may seem abstract, their implications resonate deeply in the intricate tapestry of human connection. This subchapter delves into the impact of awareness, underscoring how the dissection of statistics relating to marriage can transform personal narratives, empower decision-making, and ultimately enhance the quality of romantic partnerships.

As we embark on this exploration, it's essential to recognize that each statistic tells a story. The data collected from surveys, studies, and real-life experiences paints a broader picture of relationships, revealing trends, motivations, and outcomes that can profoundly influence our understanding of love and commitment. Awareness of these facts encourages reflection, allowing individuals to confront the realities of their situations with clarity and purpose.

Consider the stunning finding that approximately 80% of marriages involve at least one partner whose motivations for entering the union lie beyond just love and commitment. This statistic alone serves as a powerful catalyst for introspection. Are you a part of this statistic, or do you believe your motivations diverge from the norm? By examining such data, individuals can better assess their own desires, intentions, and values concerning marriage. This journey begins with a critical look at the influences that shape our decisions.

Often, we are conditioned by societal narratives, familial expectations, and even romanticized portrayals of love in media to view marriage through a narrow lens. The patterns established by previous generations create a framework for our beliefs about relationships, sometimes neglecting the complexities that come with human connection. Understanding the motivations that drive people into marriage—from financial security to societal acceptance—allows us to peel back the layers of our narratives and assess whether we are acting authentically or simply conforming to external pressures.

As we cultivate our awareness regarding these statistics, we encounter a series of questions that challenge us to evaluate our stances. For example, when was the last time you reflected on your reasons for wanting to get married? Is it based on genuine love, or are you influenced by perceived necessities? Answering these questions may require uncomfortable honesty and a willingness to confront the possibility that societal expectations have tainted our understanding of love.

In addition to these reflective inquiries, this subchapter encourages the integration of interactive elements to further engage and enhance self-exploration. Reflection questions serve not merely as prompts for thought but as frameworks for actionable insights. Here are a few questions to consider:

1. What are the top three motivations behind your desire to enter a lifelong partnership?
2. How do you think societal narratives have shaped these motivations?
3. Can you identify any fears or insecurities that may be influencing your views on marriage?

By thoughtfully contemplating these questions, individuals can illuminate the often invisible threads that bind them to particular beliefs about relationships. This process catalyzes a shift from passive acceptance to proactive engagement with one's relationship goals and motivations. The added layer of quizzes can bring a more analytical perspective to self-assessment, providing insights into patterns of thought regarding marriage. For example, a quiz examining your attitudes toward commitment may reveal preconceived beliefs about love that could either align with or differ from your current desires. Such insights empower readers to understand the essence of their connections.

Another critical aspect of awareness revolves around the generational and cultural contexts in which we reside. The data regarding marriage motivations often reveals significant differences influenced by culture, age, socio-economic background, and other identity factors. For example, younger generations frequently delay marriage in pursuit of personal development, career advancement, or due to an increased emphasis on individual autonomy compared to previous generations. Understanding how these different dynamics influence personal narratives allows individuals toreposition, reject, or reevaluate traditional narratives surrounding marriage.

Variables such as divorce rates, cohabitation trends, and changing gender roles further complicate the structure of modern relationships. Recognizing these phenomena through the lens of statistics offers crucial reflections on how one's relationship might align with or diverge from broader trends. For instance, individuals may look at rising divorce rates and consider how their own decisions may—or may not—play a role in shaping the trajectory of their relationships. Awareness serves as a foundation for informed decision-making and conscious engagement with one's partner.

As we pivot toward the conclusion of this subchapter, the ultimate message is one of empowerment. Armed with knowledge about marital statistics and the ability to reflect on personal motivations, individuals are invited to take charge of their own relationship narratives. Awareness encourages an active rather than a passive approach to love, where decisions are made thoughtfully and intentions are articulated clearly.

Consider this encouraging exercise: envision a future partnership based on authenticity and shared values. What would that look like for you? This mental exercise promotes a vision of love that prioritizes connection, understanding, and mutual respect. By consciously deciding what kind of relationship you desire, you reinforce the principles of authenticity and intentional living in your commitment to love.

Engaging with the statistics of marriage helps demystify the often convoluted narratives around love and commitment. The transformative power of awareness lies in its ability to clarify intentions, illuminate motivations, and encourage a more nuanced understanding of what it means to partner with another individual. As you continue this journey, let the statistics serve as a guide rather than a judgment—a tool that equips you to navigate the often tumultuous waters of relationships with clarity and confidence.

To further embody this shift toward awareness, here are some actionable steps you can take:

1. Keep a Relationship Journal: Document your thoughts, reflections, and feelings about love, marriage, and your personal experiences. Over time, you can discern patterns and gain deeper insights into your motivations.

2. Engage in Open Conversations: Share what you've learned from the statistics and reflect on them in discussions with your partner or close friends. This dialogue fosters collective awareness and

encourages growth within your relationships.

3. Attend Workshops or Counseling: Consider engaging with marriage workshops or relationship counseling that focuses on these statistics and personal motivations. Participating in guided discussions allows for communal learning and reflection.

Ultimately, fostering awareness lays a solid foundation for healthy relationships. It enhances emotional intelligence, deepens connections, and leads to a more fulfilling partnership grounded in understanding rather than assumption. Knowledge becomes an essential weapon against disillusionment and disappointment, empowering individuals to cultivate relationships that are not merely convenient but rich in love and authenticity.

As we conclude this exploration of awareness and its impact on personal narratives, remember that the journey toward a rewarding and thriving relationship is ongoing. Embrace the insights gained, reflect on your unique narrative, and remain open to the lessons that lie ahead. The road to love and commitment may be fraught with challenges, but equipped with knowledge, you have the power to navigate it with grace and purpose.

The Psychology of Love

Emotional Needs and Relationship Dynamics

In understanding love and commitment, it is essential to delve into the emotional needs that underpin our relationships. Human beings are complex creatures, driven by a range of psychological factors, many of which manifest in our romantic encounters. The emotional landscape of our relationships often dictates how we connect with our partners—or fail to. Issues such as security, validation, and intimacy emerge as critical elements in forging meaningful connections, but when these needs go unmet, they can lead to significant conflict and disconnection. This subchapter aims to explore these emotional needs, their impact on relationship dynamics, and how failure to address them can jeopardize our unions.

At the heart of our emotional needs is the quest for security. Throughout our lives, many of us grow to equate love with safety. This connection begins in childhood, where the emotional security provided by caregivers forms the basis for our future relationships. When we feel secure, we are more likely to engage openly and honestly with our partners, allowing for deeper emotional intimacy. Conversely, when insecurity pervades a relationship, it exerts a stifling influence, breeding doubt and fear.

Take the case of Jenna and Mark. Together for several years, they appeared to embody the ideal partnership. However, beneath the surface, Mark struggled with insecurities stemming from his upbringing. Raised in a household where parental support was often conditional, he had internalized a fear of rejection. This fear manifested in constant neediness toward Jenna, creating a one-sided emotional dynamic. Mark's inability to communicate his insecurities in a constructive manner led Jenna to feel overwhelmed. She began to withdraw, seeking space as she grappled with Mark's insistence on maintaining a constant emotional connection. What began as a genuine desire for security morphed into the suffocating presence of dependency.

As the months progressed, both Jenna and Mark found themselves continually at odds. Mark's emotional need for reassurance conflicted with Jenna's need for independence, revealing the complex interplay of emotional needs that can define a relationship. Instead of forging a deep emotional bond, they found themselves tangled in cycles of conflict, each partner's unmet needs pushing the other further away. Counselors often refer to this dynamic as the "pursuer and distancer" pattern, underscoring how two individuals can unintentionally create opposing forces that compromise their relationship.

Validation is another critical emotional need that plays a pivotal role in relationship dynamics. We all seek validation in various areas of our lives, but this need often takes center stage in romantic partnerships. When our emotional contributions are acknowledged and affirmed, we feel valued and accepted. In contrast, the absence of validation can leave individuals feeling insignificant and isolated.

Consider Laura and Tom, a couple who seemed to have it all figured out. Both successful in their careers, they shared numerous interests and enjoyed spending time together. Yet, Laura often found herself feeling unfulfilled. While Tom was adept at articulating his opinions and achievements, he rarely acknowledged Laura's accomplishments or emotional contributions. This lack of validation began to weigh heavily on Laura, who felt that her voice was silenced within the relationship.

As time passed, Laura's frustration grew, leading her to withdraw emotionally. She sought recognition from friends and colleagues, but that external validation could not quell the desire for acknowledgment from Tom. Rather than venturing into difficult discussions, Laura chose to bury her feelings, creating a chasm that increasingly separated them. Tom, oblivious to Laura's emotional turmoil, continued his patterns, unaware of the impact that his actions—or lack thereof—were having on their relationship.

This dynamic underscores how unmet emotional needs can foster resentment and create distance. In healthy relationships, both partners actively work towards validating each other's experiences and emotions. However, when one partner remains oblivious to the other's needs, the foundational trust that unites them can quickly erode.

Intimacy is the third crucial emotional need that shapes relationships, encompassing both physical closeness and emotional vulnerability. While physical intimacy often garners attention, emotional intimacy entails a deeper connection—expressing fears, glories, and insecurities. When both forms of intimacy flourish, relationships thrive. However, neglecting intimacy could leave partners feeling alienated in the very bond that should unite them.

Consider the story of Alex and Mia. They were often praised for their chemistry, exuding warmth and affection that drew others to them. However, beneath the veneer of a flawless relationship lay a deeper issue: Alex struggled with articulating his feelings. As the months wore on, Mia grew increasingly frustrated by his emotional reticence. Alex adored Mia, yet was locked in a cycle of self-doubt, worried about being vulnerable. Over time, his reluctance to share deeper emotions left Mia feeling an emotional void.

Faced with this challenge, Mia began seeking emotional support in the friendships she had cultivated outside the relationship. This attempt to fulfill her intimacy need reinforced the very gap that had formed between her and Alex. Consequently, their relationship became strained, highlighting how unmet needs for intimacy can lead to resentment and emotional isolation.

It is worth noting how these emotional needs interact. Often, the unmet need for security spirals into a lack of validation, which in turn hampers intimacy. Each unmet need feeds into the next, creating a cycle of disconnection. Without proactive efforts to address these emotional needs, couples may find themselves trapped in a pattern that leads to dissatisfaction and distance.

Renowned relationship expert Dr. Susan Johnson, the founder of Emotionally Focused Therapy, emphasizes that relationship dynamics can often be understood through the lens of attachment theory. Her insights illuminate how different attachment styles—anxious, avoidant, and secure—impact the ways individuals express and negotiate their emotional needs. Those with anxious attachment often express their needs more vocally but may do so in ways that overwhelm their partners. On the other hand, individuals with avoidant attachment styles may tend to suppress vulnerabilities, leading to emotional disconnection.

Understanding these dynamics can facilitate a more empathetic awareness of not only our needs but also those of our partners. Returning to Jenna and Mark, both partners might have benefited from recognizing their differing attachment styles—Jenna's desire for independence clashing with Mark's need for reassurance—allowing for healthier conversations grounded in mutual understanding.

Similar patterns of attachment emerged in Laura and Tom's case. Had Tom understood Laura's need for validation in the context of her emotional health, he might have cultivated a more supportive dialogue while boosting her confidence. Developing an awareness of our emotional needs and those of our partners allows for deeper connection and mutual resolution of unmet needs.

There is no denying the significant role that self-awareness plays in addressing emotional needs. One of the most effective ways to cultivate understanding is through introspection. Individuals need to embark on a journey of self-discovery, seeking to understand their own emotional needs before addressing them in their relationships. This process often entails identifying patterns from previous relationships, considering how past experiences shape current behavior, and contemplating strategies toward more fulfilling connections.

In working toward self-awareness, it can be beneficial for partners to engage in open dialogue regarding their emotional needs. Partners should feel empowered to communicate what makes them feel secure, validated, and intimate. A conversation that fosters the vulnerability necessary to respectfully articulate one's needs not only brings awareness to each partner but also builds emotional safety—the ground upon which healthy relationships flourish.

However, effective communication does not guarantee immediate change. It requires ongoing effort and sensitivity to evolving emotional needs. Relationships are not static; as partners grow and change, their needs may evolve as well. A proactive approach that includes regular check-ins can help partners stay connected and mitigate potential misunderstandings before they escalate into conflict.

Implementing strategies to prioritize each other's emotional needs can engender deeper connection and fortify relationships in times of conflict. Acts of reassurance, verbal acknowledgments, and expressions of affection can all convey security, validation, and intimacy while nurturing the partnership. In principle, even small moments of emotional generosity can echo powerfully throughout a relationship.

The experiences of couples navigating these complex dynamics offer valuable lessons for understanding how emotional needs shape relationship trajectories. Each story underscores the point that acknowledging and addressing these fundamental needs is integral to nurturing lasting love and commitment. By recognizing the potential for unmet emotional needs to disrupt harmony, individuals can approach their relationships with greater empathy and openness.

Amid the struggles inherent in navigating emotional needs, there lies the opportunity for growth. Challenges in relationship dynamics present two paths: one that leads to disconnection and resentment and another that leads to deeper emotional intimacy and underlining commitment. The choice rests on recognizing, accepting, and actively addressing the interplay of these essential emotional needs. With willingness to engage with vulnerability and communicate effectively, couples stand to cultivate relationships steeped in love, acceptance, and genuine connection.

As we reflect on the power of emotional needs, we invite readers to consider their own experiences within romantic partnerships. Are there unmet needs that challenge your emotional connection? Are there patterns of disconnection that could benefit from addressing and articulating these emotional needs? In the tapestry of love, each thread weaves together the complexity of our emotional landscape, culminating in a relationship dynamic that can either flourish or falter.

Ultimately, understanding these psychological factors fosters deeper emotional engagement, transforming potential conflicts into opportunities for connection. The journey toward nurturing relationships enriched by security, validation, and intimacy is not without its challenges, but it offers the promise of profound love—one that can withstand the test of time and evolve with the changing needs of both partners. The path of understanding emotional needs is an invitation to cultivate authentic connections in a world often driven by convenience and compromise. As we embark on this journey, let us remain attuned to the emotional landscape that defines our relationships, ever willing to nurture and grow.

Past Experiences and Their Influence

In the wilderness of our emotional landscapes, past experiences linger like shadows, subtly guiding our relationship choices and shaping the dynamics we encounter in our present romantic lives. The echoes of childhood memories, the warmth of first loves, and the pangs of heartbreak weave together to create the intricate tapestry of our emotional DNA. Understanding this tapestry is essential for anyone seeking to nurture a loving and fulfilling partnership, as the wisdom gleaned from our histories often serves as the groundwork for developing healthy relationships.

Consider Sarah, a woman in her late thirties who found herself at a crossroads after her second divorce. As she sat across from her therapist, she voiced her frustration. "Why do I keep choosing the wrong partner?" she lamented. "Each time, I think it's different, but somehow, I end up in the same place—disappointed and alone." Her therapist nodded gently, encouraging Sarah to delve into the recesses of her past. Together, they explored Sarah's childhood memories, her parents' tumultuous marriage, and the inevitable fallout that marked her formative years. Each revelation unearthed a layer of understanding, illuminating how the emotional landscape of her youth played a pivotal role in shaping her romantic selections.

Sarah's story is not unique; it is a reflection of the emotional baggage many carry into their adult relationships. Our early experiences form the lens through which we view love and commitment. Positive or negative interactions with caregivers, peers, and early partners cultivate our beliefs about intimacy, trust, and vulnerability. These beliefs often echo throughout our lives, influencing who we are drawn to and how we behave in relationships.

Dr. Emily Hargrove, a clinical psychologist specializing in relationship dynamics, posits that early relationships serve as blueprints for our future romantic interactions. "The attachments we form in childhood have profound implications," she explains. "If we experienced a nurturing environment where love was given freely and openly, we're more likely to seek partners who embody those qualities. Conversely, if our early experiences were marked by neglect or inconsistency, it can lead to anxious or avoidant attachment styles that manifest in unhealthy behaviors or relationship choices."

This notion of attachment styles is foundational in understanding how past experiences inform our present relationships. Adults with secure attachment styles often foster open communication and emotional sharing in their romantic partnerships. In contrast, those with anxious attachment may find themselves constantly seeking reassurance and validation, while avoidant individuals may create emotional distance, fearing intimacy.

Let's explore the narrative of David, who grew up in a household where emotional expression was stifled. His father, a stoic figure, believed that vulnerability was a sign of weakness, while his mother oscillated between affection and withdrawal, leaving David with confusion about love and commitment. As an adult, David gravitated towards relationships that echoed his childhood experiences. He often found himself with partners who were emotionally unavailable, repeating a cycle of yearning for closeness yet recoiling when it made him feel uncomfortable.

David's story illustrates the paradox of our pasts: we often subconsciously replicate dynamics we've known, even when those dynamics are unhealthy. Reflecting on his experiences, David acknowledged, "I didn't even realize I was doing it until I started to really look at my relationships. It's like I was drawn to it—they felt familiar, but not in a good way." Through therapy and self-reflection, David began to recognize the patterns he had created and actively sought to break free from the chains of his past.

Understanding these emotional patterns is crucial for fostering self-awareness. As individuals assess their histories, they embark on a journey toward unraveling the beliefs that dictate their choices in love. This process often involves connecting the dots between past traumas, ingrained beliefs, and current behaviors. For instance, Elena, a woman who experienced abandonment during her parents' divorce, found herself caught in a cycle of clinginess in her romantic relationships. Each time her partner left for a work trip, she spiraled into anxiety, fearing they would disappear for good. It took time, introspection, and the guidance of a skilled therapist for Elena to realize that her emotional responses were rooted in her childhood fears of abandonment.

The transformative journey of self-awareness is often enriched by poignant anecdotes—stories shared in therapy or conversations with trusted friends that resonate and offer validation. "If I hadn't talked about my past with someone, I might still be in that same pattern," Elena reflected, acknowledging the significance of sharing her experiences with others. "Sometimes, just hearing I say it out loud helps put things into perspective." The act of vocalizing our histories can provide clarity, enabling us to reframe our narratives and empower ourselves in making conscious choices in relationships.

It is also within these narratives that we find common ground with others. Groups or community spaces where individuals share their relationship experiences provide a platform for connection and healing. As we listen to others recount their struggles, we often discover that our fears and insecurities are not unique but rather part of the shared human experience. It's this collective understanding that fosters empathy and encourages us to forge deeper connections based on authenticity and vulnerability.

The creating of a secure emotional foundation in marriage demands introspection and effort. It is essential to recognize that our pasts are not prisons; rather, they can serve as tools for growth. By understanding the influences of childhood experiences and previous relationships, we can approach future partnerships with renewed clarity. This understanding cultivates a sense of agency—the power to navigate love with greater awareness and intention.

As we journey through life, the importance of emotional scaffolding becomes evident. Relationships built on the understanding of individual histories nurture an environment of compassion and acceptance. Couples who engage in these discussions often find that they develop a deeper connection rooted in empathy. For instance, when partners openly communicate their fears, past pain, and insecurities, they not only build trust but also co-create a safe space where both individuals can flourish.

Imagine a couple—Mark and Julie—who were both in the process of unpacking their past experiences as they prepared to take the leap into marriage. During one of their deep conversations, they discovered shared wounds from past relationships. Mark recounted a painful breakup, where betrayal shattered his trust. Julie spoke about her parents' tumultuous relationship and how it left her wary of commitment. Each recounting became a bridge rather than a barrier—a shared understanding that deepened their bond.

Their ability to express vulnerability allowed Mark to support Julie in working through her fears and prompted her to reassure him of her commitment. "It was liberating," Mark later confessed. "Once we understood each other's fears, it felt less like I was fighting against her insecurities and more like we were a team navigating the unpredictable waters together."

Moreover, the journey of understanding one's past fosters emotional resilience. When we acknowledge our histories, we also acknowledge our capacity to heal and transform. The stories we tell ourselves about our past relationships play a crucial role in defining our current interactions. If we view our past as a series of failures, we may enter new relationships through a lens of apprehension, expecting hurt and disappointment. Conversely, viewing our past as an opportunity for learning allows us to approach love with hope, curiosity, and a willingness to grow.

As the narrator reflects on this transformative journey, it becomes evident that the path to emotional maturity involves integrating our past experiences into our present identities. Each heartbreak and lesson learned shapes us, crafting a more profound understanding of love, patience, and acceptance. It breeds the resilience necessary to face the inevitable challenges of marriage, inviting couples to shift from a mindset of defensiveness to one of collaboration.

Additionally, self-awareness incorporates recognizing the differences in emotional reactions that may arise in partnership dynamics. As individuals grow more attuned to their triggers and motivations, they can express their needs constructively and create a space for their partners to do the same. In turn, this enhances emotional intimacy and fortifies the bond between partners. For example, Nathan, who often found himself withdrawing during conflicts, began to communicate his need for space without shutting down completely. He shared, "Understanding my triggers helped me articulate what I needed instead of retreating into silence. It made a big difference in how we resolved issues."

As we delve into the narratives of others, it's crucial to remember that our pasts don't have to dictate our futures. Although they shape us, they do not define us. The accounts of individuals navigating the intricacies of their histories reveal a simple truth: personal evolution is possible. Many have emerged from the struggles of their pasts to foster relationships marked by acceptance, trust, and genuine love.

Through stories of growth, we see people reinforcing

their self-awareness as they confront past trauma. Maria, an individual who had experienced emotional abuse in a previous relationship, worked tirelessly to rebuild her sense of self-worth. Through therapy and a supportive community, Maria learned to recognize the patterns that sought to undermine her confidence. This knowledge empowered her to ultimately establish a loving relationship, built on mutual respect and equality. "I never thought I could trust again, but understanding where my fears came from allowed me to see they were just reflections of my past, not my future," she reflected.

This notion serves as a beacon of hope for anyone feeling burdened by their history. It reminds us that understanding and healing are available no matter where we come from. The stories of people like Maria underscore that transformation is not only possible; it is a testament to the resilience inherent to the human experience. As we explore the impact of past experiences, we reveal the potential for renewal and growth, even when the shadows of the past loom large.

Central to the essence of cultivating a healthy relationship is the willingness to engage in continuous self-reflection and exploration. Understanding our individual histories and the accompanying emotions offers an apt opportunity for self-improvement. The goal is not merely to recognize our patterns but to enact change—creating relationship dynamics that reflect growth rather than stagnation.

Through this journey of self-discovery, individuals learn to embrace the complexities of love and commitment. They cultivate skills in communicating their needs and fears, allowing for the establishment of healthy boundaries. The vulnerability that comes with sharing intimate parts of oneself—coupled with the support and acceptance from partners—becomes a source of strength, not weakness.

Ultimately, the endeavor to recognize and understand the influences of our past experiences brings us closer to the love we seek. It inspires a deeper connection rooted in empathy, authenticity, and mutual understanding. As we unpack our unique histories, we draw from the wellspring of knowledge that empowers us to navigate love with intention and awareness.

In the intricate dance of relationships, it is essential to foster a mindset that views personal growth as a lifelong journey rather than a destination. Each effort made toward understanding oneself brings couples a step closer to the deep emotional intimacy they desire. As we embrace our pasts, we begin to craft partnerships founded on authenticity and mutual respect, carving a path toward relationships rich with love that transcends mere convenience.

Thus, in recognizing the significance of our past experiences, we cultivate the wisdom necessary for building secure emotional foundations in marriage. Through deliberate reflection and shared stories, we learn to navigate the complexities of love with confidence and grace, stepping boldly into the transformative power of commitment joyfully and authentically.

The Path to Emotional Maturity

Emotional maturity plays a crucial role in the health and longevity of relationships. By fostering emotional maturity, individuals cultivate the ability to navigate interpersonal dynamics with empathy, understanding, and a sense of responsibility. The journey towards emotional maturity is not just beneficial for the individual; it serves as a vital foundation for nurturing strong, loving relationships. This subchapter explores the pathways to emotional maturity and offers practical advice on developing emotional intelligence and effective communication skills.

At the heart of emotional maturity lies emotional intelligence, which encompasses several key components: self-awareness, self-regulation, motivation, empathy, and social skills. Each of these elements contributes uniquely to creating a stable emotional environment within relationships. When individuals understand their own feelings and communicate them effectively, they pave the way for deeper connections with partners.

Self-awareness is the first step towards emotional maturity. It involves recognizing one's own emotions, understanding how they influence thoughts and behaviors, and being capable of reflecting on reactions in various situations. An emotionally mature person can identify feelings such as anger, frustration, joy, or sadness and understand the underlying reasons for these emotions. For instance, if an individual feels neglected in a relationship, recognizing this feeling and understanding its origins can lead to constructive conversations with their partner rather than explosive outbursts that may damage the relationship.

Developing self-awareness requires a commitment to introspection and reflection. Methods such as journaling can be beneficial. Keeping a daily journal allows individuals to track their emotions, thoughts, and behaviors over time.

Not only does this promote self-reflection, but it also helps identify patterns in emotional responses. Regularly revisiting these notes can foster greater understanding of oneself and one's emotional triggers. Similarly, practicing mindfulness can enhance self-awareness. Mindfulness techniques, such as meditation or mindful breathing, enable individuals to remain present and aware of their emotions without judgment. This practice can create a space in which one can observe emotions as they arise, leading to better management of feelings.

Once individuals cultivate self-awareness, the next step is self-regulation. This involves managing one's emotions effectively, especially when faced with stress or conflict. A key aspect of self-regulation is learning to respond rather than react. Many people find themselves in heated moments, where they say or do things they later regret. Emotional maturity allows individuals to take a step back, breathe, and assess the situation before responding. For example, if an argument arises over household responsibilities, rather than reacting defensively, an emotionally mature individual might express their feelings calmly and discuss solutions collaboratively.

Self-regulation can be practiced through techniques that promote patience and calmness, such as deep breathing exercises or taking a break during an argument to allow emotions to settle. Understanding personal coping mechanisms is also a component of self-regulation. Whether it involves physical activities, listening to music, or engaging in creative pursuits, individuals should identify healthy coping strategies to manage stress effectively.

Another essential element of emotional maturity is

motivation. This goes beyond mere personal ambition or goals; in the context of relationships, it refers to the inner drive to cultivate and maintain meaningful connections. Emotionally mature individuals recognize the value of their relationships and are motivated to nurture them actively. This motivation may manifest as investing time in each other, prioritizing open communication, or advocating for each other's needs in times of stress.

Motivation in relationships is closely tied to the ability to see a partner's perspective and to empathize with their feelings and experiences. Empathy, the ability to understand and share the feelings of another, is a cornerstone of emotional maturity. In a world where it can be all too easy to become self-focused, empathy encourages individuals to consider their partner's emotions deeply. This fosters a sense of connection and belonging, as both partners feel seen and valued.

To cultivate empathy, individuals can engage in active listening, a practice that involves not only hearing the words spoken but also understanding the emotions behind them. Active listening requires full attention, avoiding interruptions, and providing feedback that denotes understanding. For instance, instead of simply nodding along while their partner speaks, an emotionally mature individual might summarize what their partner has said or ask clarifying questions. This shows genuine engagement and builds a deeper emotional bond.

Furthermore, empathy can be expanded by consciously putting oneself in another's shoes, effectively asking, "How would I feel in their situation?" Exploring contrasting emotional perspectives can help deepen connections. Role-playing scenarios or discussing hypothetical situations with other friends or family can enhance this process, allowing individuals to expand their capacity for empathy in varied contexts.

Social skills are another crucial aspect of emotional maturity. These skills encompass both verbal and non-verbal communication, including understanding body language and emotional cues. As individuals engage with their partners, being attuned to these subtle signals can prevent misunderstandings. For example, if a partner appears withdrawn during a conversation, recognizing this body language can prompt inquiries about their feelings, fostering an open dialogue that addresses potential issues before they fester.

Moreover, mastering conflict resolution is a vital social skill that contributes to emotional maturity. Conflict is inevitable in any relationship, but it is how couples navigate these disagreements that can define the strength of their bond. Emotionally mature individuals understand that conflict need not lead to destruction but can serve as a catalyst for growth. They approach disagreements as opportunities for understanding rather than battles to be won.

Effective conflict resolution involves several strategies: remaining calm, focusing on the issue at hand rather than personal attacks, and being willing to compromise. Finding common ground can turn conflicts into collaborative problem-solving sessions. For instance, if partners disagree on how to manage finances, emotionally mature individuals discuss their perspectives openly and seek mutually beneficial solutions that respect the needs and concerns of both parties.

It is also essential to acknowledge the role that vulnerability plays in emotional maturity. Opening one up to another person can be daunting, especially if past experiences have led to hurt or disappointment. However, allowing oneself to be vulnerable fosters deeper intimacy. Vulnerability invites partners to confide in one another, share personal stories, and express their fears or insecurities. This exchange builds trust and demonstrates a level of emotional investment that can strengthen a relationship.

Building vulnerability involves taking small steps. Begin by sharing thoughts or feelings about less sensitive topics and gradually work towards deeper emotional sharing. Celebrating the act of being vulnerable can further enhance emotional intimacy, creating a safe space for both partners to express themselves authentically. Couples may find it useful to schedule regular "check-ins," where both partners can discuss their emotional states, needs, and any concerns in a supportive and open environment.

While the journey toward emotional maturity is highly individualized, there are universal principles that can guide individuals on their path. Professionals in the field of relationship counseling suggest ongoing self-education as a crucial aspect of emotional growth. Reading books, attending workshops, or seeking couples' therapy can provide valuable insights into relationship dynamics and personal development.

Online courses are another excellent option for those seeking to develop emotional intelligence and communication skills. Many platforms offer workshops on active listening, empathy, and conflict resolution, allowing individuals to work at their own pace while gaining valuable knowledge to use within their relationships.

Fostering a growth mindset also contributes to emotional maturity. This perspective encourages individuals to view challenges as opportunities to learn rather than failures. The ability to embrace setbacks and learn from mistakes is critical in relationships, where miscommunication and misunderstandings are bound to occur. Having the courage to accept imperfections and gaps in emotional understanding encourages partners to work through difficulties together, ultimately leading to greater intimacy and connection.

Mentorship and peer support can also aid the journey toward emotional maturity. Seeking guidance from trusted friends or mentors who model strong emotional maturity can provide inspiration and actionable advice. Engaging in open discussions about relationship struggles reinforces the idea that emotional growth is not a solitary journey; instead, it flourishes within communities of support.

A significant element of emotional maturity is fostering accountability. Each partner should take ownership of their actions and feelings. Assigning blame for relationship problems only leads to resentment and defensiveness. Emotionally mature individuals recognize that both partners are responsible for maintaining a healthy relationship. This realization often necessitates an honest self-assessment regarding how personal actions impact the relationship dynamic.

Finally, take actionable steps to reinforce emotional maturity continuously. Small habits can lead to lasting change when consistently practiced. Regularly express gratitude towards one's partner, acknowledging their efforts and contributions. Proactively seek opportunities for emotional connection, such as engaging in shared hobbies, regular date nights, or new experiences that strengthen the partnership.

In conclusion, the path to emotional maturity is a rich, ongoing journey that requires dedication, self-reflection, and the willingness to engage deeply with oneself and one's partner. By fostering self-awareness, self-regulation, empathy, effective communication, and accountability, individuals create stable emotional environments that foster connection, intimacy, and mutual support.

Developing emotional intelligence is not only essential for individual growth but also crucial to nurturing lasting, loving relationships. Encouragingly, this journey towards emotional maturity is not meant to be taken alone; instead, it thrives in the shared experiences fostered by trust and mutual support. As readers embark on this journey, remember that each step towards emotional maturity paves the way for deeper connections and greater fulfillment in love and partnership, enriching both individual lives and their relationships.

Red Flags and Early Signs

Recognizing the Signs

In the realm of romantic relationships, the onset of discontent can be deceptively subtle, often cloaked in the familiarity of daily life. Those who have experienced a gradual decline in happiness may attest to the disorienting feeling of watching a once-vibrant connection fade into an uneasy silence. Relationships thrive on communication, trust, and shared experiences, but when these elements erode, signs of potential betrayal or discontent can surface in ways that challenge our perceptions and instincts.

In this subchapter, we will delve into the early warning signs that often precede deeper issues in relationships, shedding light on the common red flags that can manifest in daily interactions. By recognizing these indicators, readers can cultivate a sense of awareness that empowers them to address concerns before they escalate into crises.

One of the most critical aspects of detecting early signs of discontent is to trust one's instincts. As 'The Advocate' reminds us, intuition plays a vital role in our understanding of emotional dynamics. If something feels off in a relationship, it warrants attention. Often, individuals may dismiss their feelings, chalking them up to insecurity or paranoia. However, paying attention to these gut feelings can navigate us away from unwanted heartache.

Communication is the cornerstone of any relationship, and a noticeable decline in open dialogue can signal trouble ahead. For instance, consider the story of

Emily and Jake, a couple who appeared to be the picture of happiness. Friends marveled at their chemistry, but beneath the surface, a rift was developing. Emily noticed Jake seemed increasingly distracted during their conversations. He would nod at her words but seldom engaged, his mind seemingly elsewhere. What had once been lively discussions now felt barren and rehearsed.

Such behavior is often a significant red flag. When partners neglect meaningful exchanges, it can indicate an emotional withdrawal. Conversations should flow freely; when they become one-sided or shallow, something deeper often lurks beneath the surface. The warm connection that binds partners can fray when communication dwindles. As 'The Advocate' points out, early intervention is essential. Couples need to express concerns before those small gaps in communication widen into chasms of misunderstanding.

Another warning sign to consider is the shift in physical affection. Intimacy is integral to emotional closeness, and when it begins to fade, it can ignite concerns about one partner's feelings. For instance, Laura found herself increasingly perplexed when her husband, Mark, stopped initiating touch. Initially, they were affectionate and playful, often cuddling on the couch and holding hands during evening walks. Yet, as time passed, Laura felt the void growing. The sweet gestures diminished into a distant memory, replaced by a routine that felt mechanical.

Lack of physical affection isn't just about missing the touch but can symbolize a more significant emotional disengagement. It is crucial for partners to openly discuss their needs regarding physical and emotional intimacy. Ignoring this change can lead to unresolved feelings of neglect or resentment. Laura's story reflects the importance of addressing the issue with Mark directly, steering conversations towards finding a balance that satisfies both partners.

Additionally, patterns of avoidance can manifest as early warning signs. When one partner begins dodging discussions about issues in the relationship, it serves as a signal for concern. Rebecca noticed an inconsistency with her boyfriend, Sam. At first, every conversation about their future was met with excitement, but now Sam suddenly became evasive. His reluctance to engage in serious conversations fostered an unsettling atmosphere where Rebecca persisted in questioning his commitment.

Avoidance can take many forms, such as deflecting conversations, shutting down emotionally, or shifting the topic whenever heavy issues arise. These behaviors can create anxiety within the dynamic, leaving one partner feeling disconnected and insecure. Acknowledging the presence of avoidance and directly addressing it within the relationship can prevent isolation from setting in and maintain the critical connection.

As relationships mature, expectations can become pressing. The difference between overt and subtle signs of discontent can often hinge upon unvoiced expectations. Sarah felt increasingly frustrated with her partner, Tom, who seemed indifferent to her aspirations. Whenever she shared her dreams for professional development, Tom would nod along but rarely engaged with her ideas. Instead of fostering her ambitions, he remained distant and focused on topics that held little relevance to their shared future.

In such cases, unmet expectations can morph into resentment, ultimately deteriorating the bond. Here again, 'The Advocate' stresses the importance of expressing oneself honestly and exploring how expectations align between partners. Articulating what each person envisions for their future can reinforce commitment while successfully navigating potential differences.

An additional warning sign of unrest can emerge through behavior changes that signal emotional disconnection. For example, Lily and Jason started as inseparable partners, sharing meals and making plans together. However, after Jason began prioritizing social gatherings with friends over their time together, Lily felt sidelined. The sudden shift in behavior left her questioning whether their relationship still held value in his life.

Such changes can often reflect deeper feelings of discontentment. Partners must stay attuned to signs of withdrawal or disengagement. Lily chose to confront Jason about her feelings, sparking a conversation that revealed Jason felt overwhelmed with responsibilities and sought comfort in social support. It emphasized how crucial it is to address behavior shifts early, rather than allowing them to fester into emotional barriers.

Personality shifts are another reliable indicator that someone may be struggling internally. Changes in attitude, such as increased irritability, withdrawal, or hostility, can often be a reflection of internal conflict. Matthew noticed his girlfriend, Diana, becoming increasingly critical and pensive. The compassionate nature that initially drew him to her now felt replaced with an undercurrent of frustration.

Recognizing these personality changes is essential rather than permitting them to signal a rift in the relationship. As 'The Advocate' notes, encouraging open dialogue about feelings can often reveal unexpected sources of distress. In Diana's case, conversations with Matthew uncovered her struggles at work, helping to diffuse the tensions that had arisen.

Checking in on how each partner experiences emotional well-being is vital. Relationships require emotional labor, often manifesting as physical or mental exhaustion in one partner. If stress remains unaddressed, it can inadvertently project onto the relationship and cause strain. Partners must prioritize mutual support to weather life's challenges, strengthening their bond amid external pressures.

Another inventory of red flags includes a withdrawal from shared interests or activities. When one partner disengages from situations that once brought them joy, it can signal an emotional disconnect. Jamie had always loved cooking together with his partner, Alex, but recently noticed that Alex appeared uninterested in preparing meals. The shared ritual became void of warmth when it was often met with resistance. Jamie began to sense a barrier forming, worrying whether Alex had grown tired of their life together.

This form of emotional withdrawal can extend beyond shared interests, reflecting a more profound sense of dissatisfaction. Using this opportunity to confront Alex about the changes, Jamie expressed his feelings about their routine. This led to a re-engagement in their previous activities and rekindled passion.

The presence of dishonesty, whether big or small, is often a signal that should never be ignored. Fostering trust takes time, yet breaches of honesty can shatter the foundation of a relationship. For example, Claire found herself increasingly anxious about her partner, Derek, who frequently "forgot" details of their plans. What seemed initially harmless evolved into scenarios where she discovered he wasn't transparent about spending time with others when he said he would be elsewhere.

Encouraging open discussions about honesty is crucial for fostering trust. Relationships should be anchored in transparency where partners feel safe sharing vulnerabilities. When dishonesty exists, it is imperative to address it before it grows into the cracks of mistrust.

The manifestation of jealousy is another aspect to be vigilant about in romantic partnerships. While a little jealousy may be expected, extreme or controlling behaviors can indicate an underlying insecurity. Tanisha felt smothered by her partner's constant inquiries into her whereabouts. At first, it appeared sweet, but soon began to escalate. His behavior led Tanisha into a suffocating space where she felt unable to engage with friends without fear of provoking his jealousy.

Jealousy can erode the very fabric of intimacy. Conversations about feelings and boundaries are essential. Tanisha took the opportunity to confront her partner and find a common understanding, addressing the negative impacts of jealousy head-on to restore healthy dynamics.

As we assess red flags, it is also worth noting that

friends and family often provide invaluable insight into the state of a relationship. Close confidants may notice changes that, in the rush of daily life, partners overlook. For Michael, a visit from his brother provided clarity that he might have missed. His brother noted the tension in his exchanges with Samantha, pointing out the negative energy that had become part of their interactions.

Taking time to seek external perspectives can shed light on evolving dynamics, prompting reflection and discussion. Whether through a trusted friend or therapist, working through observations can lead to improved dialogue and understanding.

Lastly, it is crucial to emphasize the necessity of prioritizing one's emotional well-being when navigating early signs of discontent. Sometimes, recognizing the signs may lead to the realization that the relationship no longer aligns with one's core values or aspirations. In this case, individual introspection becomes paramount.

Finding fulfillment should supersede the need to preserve a failing relationship. Sarah learned this lesson when she recognized that the emotional toll of her relationship with Eric outweighed the pleasant memories. By focusing on her well-being and personal growth, Sarah opened herself to new possibilities beyond her experience with Eric.

Building self-awareness nurtures emotional intelligence, reinforcing the notion that addressing red flags should not be an exercise in blame but an opportunity for growth. 'The Advocate' affirms that both partners must engage positively, bolstering their ability to confront challenges collaboratively, reinforcing that navigating these complexities can ultimately release partners from unhealthy dynamics.

In conclusion, recognizing the signs of discontent in relationships is a vital skill for any individual navigating the complex landscape of love. From communication breakdowns to shifts in intimacy, red flags are often signals beckoning attention. By trusting instincts and entering conversations with curiosity and openness, partners can address concerns that arise before they develop into insurmountable barriers. As relationships weave through life's ebbs and flows, maintaining vigilance toward emotional health ensures partners can celebrate authentic, meaningful connections rather than succumb to the perils of discontent and betrayal.

The Stories Behind the Signs

As the sun dipped below the horizon, casting a warm orange hue across the living room, Sarah sat on her couch, her mind racing with memories of the past few years. The pillows were still arranged where they had sat during countless discussions, arguments, and tender moments shared with Jason, her husband of three years. But lately, the conversations had grown more strained, the tenderness had faded, and the laughter that once filled the space now echoed with silence.

Only a year prior, Sarah recalls the thrill of their engagement—a whirlwind romance that had felt like a fairy tale. She had met Jason at a mutual friend's wedding, and he had swept her off her feet with his charm and charisma. He was handsome, successful, and seemed genuinely interested in her life. But in hindsight, Sarah realizes the signs had been there all along—the small irritations, the dismissive comments when she shared her thoughts and feelings, the way he would often prioritize his own needs over hers. At the time, she had rationalized these red flags, attributing them to his high-pressure job or dismissing them as minor quirks.

"I thought love was enough to conquer any challenge," she reflects, her voice tinged with regret. "I was so blinded by the fantasy of our relationship that I ignored the reality of who he was." The emotional weight of her insights resonates deeply, pressing against her chest as she remembers the day she discovered Jason's infidelity. It was a rainy Thursday evening when she stumbled upon a series of messages between him and a woman she had never heard of. Each notification on his phone sent a fresh wave of anxiety coursing through her veins until she could no longer deny the truth.

Across town, Mark faced his own reckoning. He had always considered himself a pragmatic man, someone who approached love as a partnership rooted in respect and mutual support. But when he started dating Elena, he found himself enchanted by her vivacity and energy. She was the life of every party and held a magnetic pull that drew everyone in. From the outset, Mark was aware of her occasional impulsiveness, her tendency to drown out the voices of reason in favor of spontaneous adventures.

"The first time I noticed something was off was when she asked me to skip work to join her for a last-minute trip to the beach. It was fun at the time, but soon it escalated to cancelling plans and disregarding our agreed-upon boundaries," he reflects, his brow furrowing in thought. "I remember thinking, 'She's just young and carefree. It's not a big deal.' But deep down, I felt a nagging voice warning me that her unpredictability could damage our relationship."

Elena's reckless behavior became increasingly frequent, yet Mark brushed it aside as an aspect of her persona that would eventually stabilize. He was captivated by how dazzling she looked when she laughed, a stark contrast to the nagging thoughts nagging at his conscience. When her habits spiraled out of control, Mark found himself caught between admiration and frustration, ultimately silencing his discomfort.

Months later, indulging in the allure of fleeting moments, Mark found himself in a relationship marked by emotional neglect and disregard for mutual respect. The implications of that negligence culminated in a heart-wrenching breakup, leaving him feeling hollow, wondering why he hadn't recognized earlier that the very behavior he once thought was charming had spiraled into an emotional rollercoaster that he didn't know how to escape.

Meanwhile, Laura, a vibrant and ambitious woman in her late twenties, had always prioritized her career over romantic relationships. Love had seemed like an unnecessary distraction until she met Eric. He was intelligent, witty, and just as career-driven as she was. The initial joy of their relationship was intoxicating, yet with each passing day, the small things began to gnaw at her—the subtle digs about her ambitions being too lofty, the dismissive gestures when she shared her plans, and the passive-aggressive comments about her late nights at the office.

"I remember feeling this unease every time he made a joke about how I was 'married to my job,'" Laura recalls, her voice revealing a layer of vulnerability she rarely allowed others to see. "But I laughed it off. I didn't want to admit that his jokes struck a nerve. I wanted to believe he supported me. After all, he was so charming and accomplished. The way he carried himself made me feel like I had finally met someone who understood me."

Laura brushed aside the signs until everything came crashing down. The relationship spiraled into a power struggle marked by Eric's subtle efforts to undermine her successes, culminating in the day he outright told her that she would never be as successful as he was. "In that moment, I realized that I had overlooked so many red flags. I had allowed myself to believe that love could blind us to incompatibilities, but the emotional fallout was brutal," she says, tears welling in her eyes.

The stories of Sarah, Mark, and Laura serve as poignant reminders of the emotional turmoil that can erupt from ignoring the early signs of dissatisfaction and betrayal. In each case, the individuals wrestled with their own internal conflicts, questioning their feelings of regret while simultaneously trying to make sense of their experiences. As readers journey through their narratives, it becomes clear that the emotional landscapes they navigated reflect the struggles many encounter in their relationships.

The regret that lingers in Sarah's heart is palpable as she reflects on the moments she brushed aside. "I didn't want to come off as needy or insecure, so I chose to ignore the small betrayals of trust—the way he would cancel plans at the last minute or take calls in another room. But when I found out he was seeing someone else, I realized I had neglected my own needs for the sake of keeping peace," she confesses.

Similarly, Mark's reflections lead him to question his identity in the relationship. "I modified my priorities for her whims, thinking it would foster mutual happiness. I let my gut feelings quiet down with the illusions of love. Now, I see how dangerous that was. It's made me reexamine how I show up for myself in relationships," he shares, a mixture of shame and resolve in his voice.

Throughout their stories, the trio provides readers with relatable glimpses into how dismissing emotional cues can lead to profound heartbreak. Each tale circles back to the idea that acknowledging vulnerabilities—one's own and those of their partners—is fundamental to creating a healthy relationship defined by authenticity and support.

In the backdrop of their narratives lies the importance of being vigilant about red flags: the dismissive laughter of a partner can mirror deeper insecurities, the nagging intuition of something feeling "off" can alert individuals to emotional neglect. All of these signs should serve as critical points of reflection rather than discomfort that is brushed aside. As Laura poignantly notes, "It's not that I lacked self-worth; I simply wanted to feel cherished by someone else. And that desire blinded me to the signs."

As each character wrestles with regret, they begin to reclaim their narratives, each offering readers insights into what they've learned. Sarah, having faced her truth, embarks on a healing journey, attending support group meetings where she shares her story with others who resonate with her experiences. "There's power in vulnerability," she shares with newfound strength. "Understanding that we all have scars is liberating. I'm transforming my pain into advocacy, empowering others to trust their instincts."

Mark finds solace in rediscovering his self-identity through a passion for art, one that he allowed to slip from his grasp during the relationship. "I've learned that creativity is my outlet and avenue for growth. The journey through heartbreak has ignited my desire to reconnect with myself," he says, his eyes reflecting a flicker of hope.

Laura, too, embraces a new chapter of empowerment post-relationship. "I've become an advocate for women in my professional sphere, reminding them that their ambitions are beautiful, not burdens. The one lesson I carry with me is that true love supports growth, rather than stifling it."

Through collective reflections of healing and growth, the characters underscore the reality that recognizing red flags is not solely an act of self-preservation; it is a pathway toward authentic relationships built on mutual respect and understanding.

Ultimately, the essence of their narratives revolves around the theme of self-awareness: understanding that one's needs are fundamental and should never be overlooked. Such wisdom encourages readers to examine their emotions critically, illuminating the importance of engaging with their instincts when they notice the early signs of dissatisfaction in their relationships.

As the stories culminate, readers are left with an invitation to reflect: Are they paying attention to their own red flags? Are they engaging deeply with themselves and their partners, promoting an environment of honesty and vulnerability? The emotional journey of Sarah, Mark, and Laura serves as an accessible framework for exploring the complex web of relationships—the highs, the lows, and ultimately, the paths towards reclaiming agency after neglecting the signs.

Their narratives stand as cautionary tales but also as beacons of hope, symbolizing the resilience of the human spirit. Each character emerges transformed, equipped with insights for their next relationships, ready to foster connections grounded in respect, understanding, and unwavering authenticity. It is through this lens that we come to understand the power of awareness in relationships and the strength found in navigating the complexities of love with open eyes and open hearts.

Tools for Prevention

In navigating the landscape of modern relationships, being attuned to the early signs of discontent and potential betrayal is paramount. "Tools for Prevention" aims to equip readers with proactive strategies and practical tools to address red flags and enhance open communication within their partnerships. The essence of this subchapter is to empower individuals, encouraging them to engage in meaningful dialogues about expectations and concerns before issues intensify.

One of the core aspects of a thriving relationship is the ability to communicate effectively. This requires both partners to create a safe space conducive to honest discussions. To facilitate this task, we will explore specific tools geared toward fostering open dialogues, addressing red flags early on, and promoting a nurturing relationship environment. By doing so, readers will not only learn to recognize potential issues but also develop the agency to address them proactively.

The first tool in our preventative toolkit is the "Check-In Conversation," a structured yet flexible method for opening dialogues about relationship health. This strategy emphasizes regular, intentional discussions where both partners can express their feelings, desires, and concerns without the fear of judgment or retaliation.

To implement a Check-In Conversation, set aside dedicated time each week, ideally in a relaxed, distraction-free environment. This timing can be during a quiet dinner at home or a leisurely walk in the park. The key is to make these conversations a routine part of your relationship, nurturing the habit of checking in with one another.

Begin the conversation with an invitation, such as, "I'd love to hear how you've been feeling about us this week." This opener sets the tone for a collaborative dialogue. After one partner shares their feelings, the other should actively listen without immediately offering advice or counterarguments. Engage in reflective listening by summarizing what you heard to ensure understanding: "So what I'm hearing is that you felt overwhelmed by work this week and it made you feel less connected to me. Is that right?" This technique fosters clarity and demonstrates empathy.

As part of the Check-In Conversation, incorporate

specific prompts that encourage deeper exploration of feelings. Here are some prompts to consider:

1. "What has brought you joy in our relationship this week?"
2. "Have there been any moments when you felt disconnected or frustrated?"
3. "How can we support each other better moving forward?"
4. "Are there any unfulfilled needs or desires you'd like to discuss?"

These questions should be approached with an open heart and a willingness to engage deeply. Each partner takes turns sharing and listening, validating each other's feelings in the process. By promoting regular check-ins, couples can create a culture of communication, allowing them to address small issues before they morph into larger conflicts.

Another essential tool for prevention is the use of "Red Flag Reflection Journals." A reflection journal serves as both a personal space for self-exploration and a means to facilitate conversation between partners. By maintaining this journal, individuals can track their emotions, thoughts, and patterns in their relationship over time.

To begin the journaling process, set aside time once a week to reflect on your experiences and feelings. Consider these guiding questions:

- "What emotions have I felt most strongly in our relationship this week?"
- "Have I noticed any recurring patterns that concern me?"

- "Are there specific interactions that I perceive as red flags, and how do they make me feel?"
- "What positive moments can I celebrate in our relationship?"

Writing candidly about red flags and emotional responses can illuminate underlying issues that might otherwise go unnoticed. Over time, individuals can assess patterns and trends in their relationship, identifying areas needing attention.

Once a month, schedule a time to share insights from your reflection journals with your partner during a Check-In Conversation. This integration of personal reflection with open dialogue promotes shared understanding and paves the way for constructive problem-solving. Furthermore, it signifies your commitment to individual growth and to the health of the relationship.

Communication is not just about sharing thoughts; it also includes understanding reactions. To foster greater self-awareness and empathy, couples can implement the "Feelings Wheel" exercise. The Feelings Wheel is a tool that categorizes a wide spectrum of human emotions, ranging from primary feelings like joy or anger to more complex emotions such as shame, vulnerability, or contentment.

Encourage each partner to identify their emotions using the Feelings Wheel during Check-In Conversations. By labeling feelings with specificity, partners can avoid vague expressions like "I'm fine" or "I'm upset." Instead, they can articulate, "I felt anxious and overwhelmed when you said you'd be late because it made me worry about our plans." This precise language allows partners to understand one another better and respond with greater compassion.

In addition to emotional clarity, another effective strategy is the "Expectation Mapping" exercise. Expectations often lie at the root of conflicts. When partners fail to articulate their expectations, misunderstandings arise, leading to resentment. Expectation Mapping involves collaboratively identifying and discussing expectations in various domains of the relationship, such as communication styles, conflict resolution methods, financial management, and quality time.

To perform Expectation Mapping, both partners should write down their individual expectations in each category. Consider these prompts to guide your mapping:

1. "What are my expectations for communication in our relationship?"
2. "How do I envision handling conflicts?"
3. "What does financial partnership mean to me?"
4. "What does quality time look like in our relationship?"

After sharing individual expectations, engage in dialogue about where expectations align, and where they may diverge. This dialogue can lead to clarifying discussions, helping partners establish agreements or compromises that suit both individuals.

As external factors can influence relationships, being aware of individual stressors is crucial. To address this concern, the "Stress and Support Inventory" tool comes into play. This exercise encourages partners to discuss their stressors outside the relationship and how these stressors may impact them as individuals and as a couple.

Create a joint list of individual stressors, categorized into areas such as work, family, health, or personal growth. After identifying stressors, discuss how each partner can support the other. Identifying stress point reductions or mutual support frameworks can mitigate impacts on the relationship.

For instance, if one partner is struggling at work, the other can offer emotional support through open conversations or by participating in stress-relieving activities together. Recognizing these external pressures can minimize misunderstandings and emotional disconnection, allowing for greater collective resilience.

Lastly, it is vital to incorporate "Conflict Prevention Role Plays" into your relationship toolkit. While addressing red flags and nurturing open communication is essential, it is equally crucial to prepare for inevitable conflicts or misunderstandings. Role plays allow both partners to practice responding to potential conflicts in a safe and controlled manner.

To perform a Conflict Prevention Role Play, select a hypothetical conflict scenario and take turns adopting roles while responding to the situation. This activity builds strategic communication skills and de-escalation techniques. For example, one partner may act as the individual expressing frustration, while the other practices active listening skills and emotional regulation.

Through this exercise, both partners can gain

insights into their conflict styles, learn to navigate heated moments, and rehearse de-escalation techniques, enhancing both emotional resilience and mutual understanding.

By integrating these tools into regular relationship practice, couples can foster a proactive communication culture, significantly decreasing the likelihood of red flags escalating into crises. Each tool empowers partners to recognize and address potential issues early on while also promoting emotional stewardship and responsiveness.

As you engage with these tools, remember to approach the process with a mindset of curiosity and collaboration rather than judgment or defensiveness. Sweeping issues under the rug may lead to erosion of trust and connection, but cultivating a culture of open dialogue and mutual support fosters the possibility of thriving partnerships.

Interactive elements such as worksheets, reflection prompts, and conversation starters enhance engagement, guiding readers to deepen their understanding of their relationship dynamics. Encouraging the completion of these exercises not only increases awareness but also invites individuals to take ownership of their relationship journeys.

For consistent engagement, consider creating a shared relationship calendar. Mark dates for Check-In Conversations, Expectation Mapping sessions, and reflection journal sharing. These reminders encourage commitment and accountability, reinforcing the value each partner places on cultivating a healthy emotional connection.

Fostering healthy communication and nurturing emotional safety requires dedication from both partners. As you integrate the tools presented in this subchapter, remember that building resilience and connection is an ongoing endeavor that evolves as your relationship grows. Embrace the journey, celebrate your progress, and remain open to adjusting your approaches as you learn and develop together.

In conclusion, prevention is always preferable to reaction. By implementing these proactive tools and fostering open communication, couples can navigate potential pitfalls, enhancing the long-term sustainability and fulfillment of their relationships. Equip yourself with these strategies, engage in honest conversations, and commit to nurturing genuine connections. Empower yourself to become an advocate for emotional health and relationship integrity, ensuring that you and your partner embark on a shared journey filled with love, companionship, and mutual growth. Whether you are faced with challenges or triumphs, remember that the path you tread together is one of collaboration, understanding, and unparalleled richness in love.

Real Stories, Real Lessons

A Tapestry of Experiences

In a world where the concept of marriage often feels like a fairy tale wrapped in societal expectations, real-life stories provide a powerful counter-narrative. This subchapter brings to life the voices of individuals who have traversed the often rocky terrain of partnership, highlighting not only their triumphs but also their struggles and the wisdom they've gleaned along the way. Through these eyes, we observe how love can be both an anchor and a tempest, informing the myriad choices couples make.

Our journey begins with the story of Laura and David, high school sweethearts who founded their relationship upon a deep friendship. They were the quintessential couple who everyone believed had "the perfect love." Married fresh out of college, they seemed a testament to the idea that love conquers all. Yet, beneath the surface of this idealism lay challenges that would test their bond. For Laura, the early years of marriage were marked by the pressures of societal expectation. She was determined to uphold a career while managing a household, a juggling act that often left her feeling overwhelmed.

As life settled into a rhythm, David found himself longing for the simple joys of spontaneity that characterized their early relationship. The daily grind took its toll, prompting him to feel neglected and unappreciated. Laura, in turn, felt her efforts unrecognized. Their story illuminates a critical truth: the importance of communication in nurturing a marriage. With a heart full of vulnerability, Laura opened up about her struggles during a quiet evening together. This candid conversation paved the way for a renewed understanding, allowing them to establish new traditions that honored both their aspirations and their love.

Across the country, Maria and Jorge were experiencing a very different reality. They met at a cultural festival, drawn together by a shared passion for dance and celebration. Their courtship was electric, fueled by an undeniable chemistry. Yet, as their relationship transitioned to marriage, the vibrancy of their early romance began to fade under the weight of familial expectations. Maria felt the pressure of her family's traditional values, while Jorge grappled with a desire to forge their own path. As they navigated their differences, a rift began to form.

The pivotal moment came during a family gathering. Maria overheard her mother remarking on the struggles of marriage, weaving anecdotes rich with warnings about the erosion of romance. That evening, as she reflected, it struck her how outside expectations had begun to infiltrate their bubble. With newfound resolve, she approached Jorge, expressing her fears and desires to carve out a unique identity as a couple. This moment of honesty transformed their experience. They began hosting "Culture Nights," celebrating both their heritages, reinforcing their bond while redefining love on their terms and rejecting external definitions of happiness.

Then we find ourselves with Ethan and Claire, who reported into their marriage with one expectation: adventure. Both avid travelers, they envisioned a life fuelled by exploration. However, life had other plans—Ethan was suddenly offered a prestigious job that required long hours and little flexibility. For Claire, the expansive dreams of shared wanderlust seemed to slip away as he was caught in the throes of ambition. Feeling isolated and uncertain, Claire withdrew, leading to misunderstandings soup-mired in emotional distance.

One fateful weekend, Claire decided to book a last-minute trip to a nearby city. She invited Ethan, who reluctantly agreed amidst his busy schedule, and there in the quaint charm of an unfamiliar place, they found animated conversation reigniting their cherished connection. The journey inspired a heartfelt discussion about their aspirations, not only for career but personal fulfillment, which reminded them both that love should be an expansive rather than constrictive force. They returned home with a renewed commitment to travel—this time, redefining adventure as both shared experiences and the acknowledgment of each other's needs.

Meanwhile, in a small town, we meet Sofia and Amir, a couple whose divergent backgrounds posed challenges from the very outset. Sofia was a free spirit, an artist who thrived on creativity and unpredictability, while Amir was rooted in structure and routine as an engineer. At first, their differences sparked a passionate romance filled with excitement as they challenged one another's worldviews. Yet, as the novelty wore off, the friction of their contrasting lifestyles threatened to splinter their marriage.

Through countless late-night discussions that often turned into arguments, they realized they were at a crossroads. It was during one of these exchanges when Sofia, tears streaming, confronted Amir: "Why can't you just let go and be spontaneous?" to which Amir earnestly replied, "And why can't you appreciate the stability I provide?" This critical dialogue led them to comprehend the critical aspect of compromise. They made a pact to integrate one another's styles: Sofia would schedule time for spontaneity, while Amir would create unstructured spaces in their lives. By merging their cultures, they crafted a vibrant mosaic that reflected their union—an ongoing dance of opposites.

As we shift gears, we meet Jon and Rachel, a couple who had been married for over a decade. Their relationship had weathered various storms, not least being the aftermath of a significant betrayal—an affair that had crept into their lives unexpectedly. Faced with the abyss of separation, they were forced to confront painful truths about themselves and their marriage. Rather than take the easier route of dismissing the hurt, they chose to fight for their relationship.

Jon recalls the moment he confessed to Rachel, filled with dread yet knowing honesty was their only chance for a future. Rachel, instead of reacting with anger, opted to listen. "What do you need from me?" she asked, surprised by the power of her own words. In that moment, vulnerability became the catalyst for healing. Together, they embarked on a path of intense reflection and counseling, learning the significance of forgiveness—an act that reshaped their understanding of love and partnership. Each day presented new lessons, surrendering to the idea that love is often forged in the fires of hardship, and they emerged stronger, rebuilding their foundations brick by brick.

Near the coast, Bob and Mia had created a comfortable life, yet comfort began to morph into stagnation. Over time, their connection dulled. The vibrancy they once shared seemed lost amidst late-night television and mundane routines. A catalyst for change emerged when they stumbled upon a local arts class. Motivated by a once-shared affinity for creativity, they enrolled together, unknowingly embarking on a journey that would ignite both passion and intimacy.

With each brushstroke, Bob and Mia began to communicate in ways they hadn't in years. They painted, laughed, and discovered the joy of exploring new aspects of themselves and each other. With these explorations, they reignited dialogue, communicating desires and fears long ignored. The creative outlet became a transformative vehicle for their relationship—a reminder that love flourishes when nurtured through shared experiences and passions.

In an unprecedented twist of stories, we encounter Jennifer and Mike, who represent the complexities of modern love through digital connections. Their love story began in the structured environment of an online platform. While both sought genuine connection, they were also drawn by the convenience that technology offered. However, as they moved from virtual to real-life meetings, they struggled to bridge the idealized perceptions they had formed online.

Challenges arose when Mike faced job loss, leading to feelings of inadequacy that seeped into their once light-hearted chats. Jennifer, observing his emotional turmoil, became increasingly frustrated as she felt he was withdrawing into himself, battling demons he refused to discuss. In a moment simmering with tension, she gave voice to her concerns: "I need you to be honest with me," she implored. This became a turning point that prompted Mike to seek support. Together, they learned to navigate the overlapping landscapes of vulnerability, establishing a more profound connection that transcended the convenience that once brought them together. Their experiences reflected the evolving nature of love, marked by communication that transcends the technological facade.

Finally, we meet Marcus and Lily, whose marriage had roots tied to childhood friendships. Their transition into partnership came laden with expectations based on their early bond. Yet, married life introduced a new context filled with the challenges of adult responsibilities that clashed with the playfulness that marked their youth. Each placed expectations on the other, anticipating the same spontaneity and support without open acknowledgment.

Through months of implied resentment, they undertook a "truth retreat" to reassess their priorities. Seated in nature's embrace, Marcus confided the weight of his perceived expectations, "I feel like I'm failing," he said, his voice trembling. Lily, equally apologetic, admitted, "I never wanted things to feel this heavy." This retreat marked a renewal, rooted in honesty. They committed to an experimental "creative date night" each week to explore roles beyond the confines of traditional expectations, discovering hidden aspects of one another.

As we draw upon these diverse tales, it becomes evident that every couple encounters unique trials, yet they also share common themes of vulnerability, compromise, and the importance of nurturing authentic connections. Each narrative highlighted how love is not merely an end goal but an evolving journey filled with complexities.

The lessons learned extend beyond individual stories: communication stands at the forefront, characterizing the pillars upon which successful partnerships are built. While initial motivations may differ, what allows relationships to flourish is the couples' willingness to navigate challenges with openness—a willingness to seek understanding over judgment and shared growth over individual isolation.

The tapestry of experiences weaved throughout this subchapter embodies the notion that marriage is an ever-evolving journey, steeped in history, cultural influences, shared dreams, and personal growth. Amongst the boundaries of romantic idealism, each story enriches our understanding of love, offering vital insights that resonate universally.

As we reflect on the lessons imparted, may readers find courage in the expeditions of these couples, prompts to assess their journeys and directions, and recognition that within the complex web of experiences lies the profound and transformative capacity of love. Each individual story is but a thread in a broader tapestry, inviting each reader to contribute their narrative, to learn from the past, and to embrace the future—fully illuminated by the potential of love nurtured with authenticity and care.

Lessons Learned

In the tapestry of relationships, each thread weaves

together stories of love, struggle, and discovery, revealing a rich landscape of human experience. As the various narratives unfold, certain themes emerge, guiding us toward understanding the essence of authentic love and commitment. Many individuals who have shared their journeys have illuminated profound lessons, reflecting a universal quest for connection in a world often driven by convenience and compromise. By dissecting these insights, we can forge a path toward deeper self-awareness, enabling us to nurture our relationships with empathy and intention.

One recurring lesson from these stories is the undeniable importance of authenticity. Authenticity acts as the bedrock of lasting connections, fostering trust and true intimacy. Consider the testimony of Emma and Liam, a couple who, at first glance, exemplified the picture-perfect partnership. Their life was adorned with social media highlights: romantic dinners, vacations, and a constant stream of heartwarming posts. To outsiders, their relationship seemed flawless, yet beneath the surface lay a troubling reality—both Emma and Liam struggled with their own insecurities and feelings of inadequacy, inhibiting them from presenting their true selves.

The turning point in their journey occurred during a candid conversation one evening. Emma opened up about her longing for deeper emotional connection, shedding tears while revealing her fear of never being good enough for Liam. To her surprise, Liam reciprocated with vulnerability of his own; he, too, felt pressure to appear perfect and feared disappointing Emma. This moment of shared authenticity was transformative, catalyzing a shift in their relationship dynamic. It became clear that vulnerability was not a weakness but a powerful conduit for deeper understanding and connection. By allowing themselves to be truly seen, they laid the foundation for a more authentic relationship, built on acceptance rather than idealization.

Emma and Liam's story emphasizes that authenticity is not just about being "real" with each other but also about confronting one's own fears and insecurities. It's essential in a partnership that both individuals feel safe enough to express their thoughts and feelings without the fear of judgment or rejection. The lesson here resonates deeply: vulnerability fosters connection, while the facade of perfection breeds distance and disillusionment. For readers examining their own relationships, it becomes imperative to reflect on whether they are presenting their true selves or merely a curated version influenced by societal expectations.

Another powerful theme that emerges from these narratives is the necessity of open communication. Many couples, like David and Zoe, faced significant struggles due to a lack of effective dialogue. Early in their relationship, they often glossed over conflicts in favor of maintaining peace. For months, unresolved issues simmered beneath the surface until a seemingly trivial matter escalated into an explosive argument. In the aftermath, both David and Zoe recognized that their avoidance of confrontation was damaging their bond. They realized that true love flourishes not in the absence of conflict, but through the ability to navigate disagreements productively.

With newfound determination, they committed to practicing active communication—a skill that requires effort, patience, and intention. They learned to directly address their concerns while employing empathy to understand each other's perspectives. This approach initiated a new chapter in their relationship marked by a profound sense of partnership. By embracing constructive feedback and engaging in honest conversations, they cultivated a safe space where both individuals could express themselves freely. Their story highlights the powerful reminder that an open dialogue is foundational to a thriving partnership, underscoring the necessity of addressing issues before they fester.

For readers, David and Zoe's experience encourages them to assess how they communicate with their partners. Are conflicts confronted openly, or are concerns brushed aside? The willingness to engage in honest discourse not only strengthens trust but can also nurture a deeper emotional intimacy.

The narrative of finding balance is yet another vital lesson drawn from these shared experiences. The dance of intimacy and individuality is often delicate, as highlighted in the story of Mia and Noah. In the early days of their relationship, they became so enraptured with each other that they neglected their distinct identities, interests, and friendships. Although they were inseparable, the resulting entanglement stoked feelings of resentment and stifled growth. Mia felt that her passions were being overshadowed, while Noah grappled with the pressure of being Mia's sole source of fulfillment.

Through exploration and a gradual understanding of each other's needs, they learned the importance of maintaining individuality amid togetherness. They began to prioritize both shared experiences and personal pursuits, encouraging one another to thrive independently. Time spent apart became cherished, as each cultivated their identity, ultimately enriching their connection. This story serves as a poignant reminder that while love is a powerful bond, it thrives when both partners retain their individuality. By honoring personal interests alongside their relationship, couples can strengthen their bond and create a more fulfilling partnership.

Readers are prompted to consider their own dynamics. Are they nurturing their individuality within their relationship? Embracing the importance of both connection and autonomy leads to a deeper understanding of love—a nuanced balance that invites both partners to flourish.

The stories of couples navigating the complexities of love consistently reveal another guiding principle: the value of shared values and goals. When Alex and Jo met, their instant chemistry seemed destined to blossom. However, as time unfolded, glaring differences in their values began to surface. Alex prioritized career ambitions, while Jo sought stability and family life. Despite their affection for one another, these conflicting aspirations led to misunderstandings and frustration.

It wasn't until they engaged in an open conversation about their dreams and desires that clarity began to emerge. They learned that shared life goals were essential for creating a harmonious future. By reframing their approach, Alex and Jo uncovered latent commonalities— they both craved purpose and fulfillment, albeit manifesting in different ways. Their journey highlighted the importance of alignment in values as a cornerstone of lasting commitment. Alex recognized that prioritizing family and nurturing relationships could coexist with ambition, while Jo understood the significance of pursuing personal growth.

In this story, readers are invited to examine the values they hold dear. What aspirations form the foundation of their relationships? Shared values do not equate to uniformity; rather, they establish a common ground for navigating challenges. Recognizing and embracing each person's goals and aspirations can fortify the bond between partners, steering them toward a shared vision for their future.

The narratives shared also reflect an undeniable truth: love requires effort and intention. The road to commitment is seldom linear; it is marked by sacrifices and growth, as seen in the experience of Rachel and Simon. Early in their relationship, they assumed that love alone would guide them through challenges. However, life's complexities soon began to unravel their expectations, leaving them feeling disconnected and disheartened.

During a pivotal moment of vulnerability, Rachel confessed that she felt they had become complacent. Tapped into autopilot mode, she lamented that they had stopped investing time and effort into one another. Simon initially felt defensive yet recognized the truth in her words. This sparked a marathon of conversations, resulting in a mutual commitment to rekindling their connection. Dedicating regular date nights, openly expressing appreciation, and seeking shared experiences became their new rhythm. The effort they poured into their relationship breathed new life into their bond, affirming that love requires consistent nurturing.

For readers, Rachel and Simon's journey serves as an encouraging reminder that love is not passive; it demands active participation. Reflecting on their own relationships, individuals may consider how they prioritize their partnerships. Are they investing time and intention, or have they slipped into comfortable routines? Understanding that love thrives through effort can lead to more profound and fulfilling connections.

Amidst the exploration of love and commitment, a significant theme emerges: the understanding that imperfection is an intrinsic part of the human experience. The poignant story of Julia and Mark illustrates this truth. As a couple deeply in love, they faced a significant challenge when Julia lost her job unexpectedly. The ensuing financial strain and self-doubt cast a shadow over their relationship, and Julia found herself feeling inadequate. She grappled with feelings of failure, believing that her worth was intrinsically tied to her career success.

Mark, recognizing the toll that perfectionism was taking on Julia, made it his mission to support her through this trying time. He reassured her that their love transcended societal definitions of success and failure. Their candid conversations revealed that vulnerability and support were pivotal in navigating this storm together. Instead of allowing shame to sever their bond, they cultivated compassion for one another, reminding each other that love could weather any storm. Julia's sense of purpose eventually rebounded, but the experience solidified the understanding that imperfection does not diminish worth; rather, it can illuminate the strength of love when nurtured with kindness and empathy.

For readers, Julia and Mark's journey challenges the pervasive notion that success is a precursor to love. Self-reflection on the role of perfectionism in one's relationships can lead to renewed perspectives. Embracing the flawed, human elements of partners can create an environment of resilience, where love thrives in the face of adversity.

Ultimately, the shared narratives of couples navigating love reaffirm the potency of growth, understanding, and empathy. Each story enriches the reader's ability to connect with their own experiences, illuminating the complexity of human relationships. The lessons distilled from these accounts act as guideposts, encouraging self-awareness and fostering growth.

As readers reflect on their journeys, they should consider pressing questions: Are they embracing authenticity in their relationships? Are they communicating openly and honestly? Have they cultivated individuality while nurturing connection? Are their values aligned? Are they actively participating in the journey of love? Finally, how do they embrace imperfection as a part of their shared experience?

By drawing from these poignant lessons, readers can embark on a quest for deeper connections rooted in authenticity, shared values, open communication, and mutual support. The tapestry of relationships is woven from the threads of shared stories, and it is through understanding and striving for these lessons that we can create partnerships that not only survive but flourish in complexity and depth. As each individual applies these insights, they pave the way for love that is resilient, empowering, and authentic—a journey that embraces each other as they truly are.

Sharing Insights and Building Community

In a world where individualism often reigns supreme, the importance of community and shared experiences in the realm of relationships cannot be overstated. The stories we internalize from those around us—not only from our own experiences but from the anecdotes of friends, family, or even strangers—shape our understanding of love, commitment, and the complexities that come with navigating the intricacies of partnership. These narratives act as a mirror, reflecting our own emotional landscapes, providing insights and wisdom that can help us make sense of our experiences.

Yet, in many cases, we find ourselves ensconced in silence, weathered by the fear of judgment or the vulnerability that comes with sharing deeply personal stories. This reticence can create a profound sense of isolation, one that leads us to believe that we are alone in our struggles—a sentiment that only amplifies feelings of disconnection and despair. To counteract this isolation, it is essential that we foster a culture of openness and sharing among those navigating the tumultuous waters of relationships.

One of the most enriching aspects of building a community is the opportunity to witness a diverse tapestry of experiences. Each person's journey is unique, informed by a myriad of factors including cultural backgrounds, past relationships, personal aspirations, and values. By coming together to share these stories, we uncover common threads and gain insights that are often overlooked in our solitude. These narratives become not just cautionary tales, but also sources of hope and resilience, illuminating paths forward where we once saw none.

Imagine a space where individuals feel empowered to share their relationship journeys—both the highs and lows—with unfiltered honesty. It's in this vulnerability that connections deepen, as others resonate with sentiments of heartbreak, joy, conflict, and triumph. Having a supportive community allows us to not only empathize with one another but also to draw on the collective wisdom accrued from a multitude of experiences. We learn from those who have tread similar paths, gleaning lessons that can shape our own choices and interactions.

In fostering a community centered on shared insights and experiences, we can adopt several interactive strategies to enhance this collective understanding of relationships. At its core, this involves creating environments—both online and offline—where dialogue is encouraged and celebrated. Consider organizing discussion groups or workshops focused on relationship dynamics, where participants can share their experiences in a safe and supportive atmosphere. Such gatherings foster connection while encouraging participants to reflect on their own narratives and identify patterns that may have emerged over time.

Furthermore, utilizing social media platforms to create forums for open discussion can also be immensely beneficial. Consider starting a blog or a social media group dedicated to relationship experiences and insights, where individuals can contribute stories, advice, and lessons learned. Use engaging prompts to stimulate conversation, allowing participants to express their thoughts and feelings without fear of judgment. For example, ask questions such as:

- What was a pivotal moment in your relationship that challenged your perception of love?
- Have you ever ignored red flags in a partnership? What did you learn from that experience?
- How did the community help you navigate a difficult time in your relationship?

These open-ended questions not only spark conversation but also empower individuals to engage with their experiences, promoting a deeper understanding of their own relationship dynamics.

As members of this community share their reflections, it is important to emphasize the concept of active listening. This involves not only hearing the words being spoken but also grasping the emotions and narratives behind them. When we practice active listening, we validate the experiences of others, fostering a sense of belonging and acceptance. Consider establishing a guideline within your community that encourages participants to listen with empathy and refrain from judgment.

Providing a structure for sharing experiences can also enable individuals to take turns expressing their thoughts while others listen attentively. For instance, in a discussion circle, each participant could be allotted a specific amount of time to share while others practice active listening. After everyone has had a chance to speak, the group can engage in a reflective dialogue about the insights gained. This not only enhances the sharing process but also ensures that each voice is heard and valued.

As we gather stories and insights within our community, we can create a central repository where individuals can submit their experiences anonymously, if desired. This not only allows for a broader range of narratives to be shared but can also serve as a reflective tool for others who may be grappling with similar situations. It encourages individuals to reflect on what they have learned, giving them space to articulate their growth in a way that can inspire others.

To reinforce the meaning behind these stories, consider compounding them into a biannual publication—whether in printed or digital form—that collates the wisdom shared within the community. This not only provides a tangible product that members can refer to but also acknowledges the contributions of every individual. Perhaps each edition can focus on a specific theme, such as love and vulnerability, navigating conflict, or the importance of emotional intimacy. A compilation of narratives offers encouragement to others on similar journeys, offering insights that can be invaluable as they navigate their own relationships.

Moreover, creating subcommittees or interest groups within the community to tackle specific topics related to relationships can provide focused avenues for dialogue. For example, you could form groups centered on discussions of parenting in relationships, managing finances as a couple, or supporting personal growth while in partnership. By breaking down the vast topic of relationships into manageable categories, members can further explore their unique challenges and share tailored insights.

The act of sharing insights doesn't just reside in the realm of personal experience; it also extends to lessons from literature, film, and the broader cultural discourse surrounding relationships. Encourage community members to share their favorite books or films that provide impactful insights into love and partnership. Host monthly book or movie club meetings that foster discussions about these narratives, inviting individuals to draw parallels between the fictional tales and their own lives. Such activities not only enrich the communal narrative but also engage participants in a more profound exploration of relationships.

As we cultivate community through shared insights, it's essential to maintain a focus on action and accountability. Encourage members to set personal goals based on the insights they glean from shared experiences. For instance, if a participant shares a story about successful communication strategies, others may want to adopt these techniques in their own lives. Challenge members to be accountable to one another by checking in periodically about their goals and progress.

This accountability reinforces the bonds formed within the community, as members become invested not only in their own journeys but in supporting the growth of others. It adds a tangible element of encouragement, as individuals celebrate one another's victories, big and small.

In this shared space of empathy and understanding, members can become powerful advocates for one another. Encourage them to share insights on how they can actively support friends or loved ones experiencing relational challenges. Learning how to assist others enhances the sense of community and enriches individual perspectives.

After facilitating a nurturing environment centered on shared experiences, we must recognize the importance of continuous growth and learning. Encourage members to remain curious about their relationships and to approach each interaction with an openness to learning.

Instilling a reflective mindset will help individuals navigate not only their partnerships but also the broader societal expectations tied to love and commitment. It promotes adaptability in a world that is constantly evolving. Stress that every conversation within this community—whether it's a triumphant moment or a heartbreaking revelation—contributes to their collective understanding and, ultimately, to the evolution of love itself.

As we wrap up this subchapter, let us shine a light on the invaluable role of community in transforming our relationship journeys. Each shared insight becomes a building block for understanding, empathy, and connection. The journey toward authentic love is often fraught with challenges, but it is in the solidarity of community that we find strength.

As you navigate the intricate pathways of your own relationship journeys, we invite you to actively share your stories. Create dialogues with those around you—find solace and inspiration in each other's narratives. Embrace the learning, celebrate the complexities, and, above all, cultivate a shared space that enriches and empowers every individual in their pursuit of authentic love.

Join us in the call to action. Let us build supportive networks where every voice is valued and every story serves as a guiding light. Share your experiences, engage with others, and weave an intricate tapestry of insights that can stand the test of time. By doing so, we create a community that not only understands relationships but shapes them for the better, nurturing connections that resonate with sincerity and depth.

Together, we can illuminate the often murky waters of love and partnership, celebrating the beauty that comes from collective wisdom and heartfelt engagement. The journey toward nurturing authentic relationships is not one that needs to be undertaken in isolation; it is one that thrives best in community. Embrace your voice, extend your hand, and commit to sharing insights as you navigate the adventure of love.

Building Authentic Connections

The Foundations of Authenticity

In the realm of relationships, authenticity acts as the bedrock upon which enduring connections are built. It prescribes that individuals not only express their true selves but also foster an environment where their partners feel safe and encouraged to do the same. This subchapter embarks on an exploration of the essential elements—trust, vulnerability, and emotional openness—that contribute to building authentic connections, revealing how nurturing these components can profoundly transform our interactions.

To understand the gravity of authenticity in relationships, we must first reflect on what it truly means. Authenticity is not just about being true to oneself; it also involves acknowledging the complexities of our human experiences and imperfections. In relationships, authenticity invites a level of honesty that transcends superficial interaction, pushing us into the realm of profound connection. It empowers partners to share their fears, aspirations, and vulnerabilities without the haunting fear of judgment or retribution.

Consider the story of Mia and James, a couple who epitomized the struggle for authenticity. Initially, their relationship was defined by light-hearted banter and surface-level conversations. They enjoyed each other's company, but their interactions mostly revolved around trivial matters and shared hobbies, avoiding deeper issues such as their familial struggles or personal insecurities.

As time passed, life began to throw challenges at them. James found himself facing professional setbacks, and Mia grappled with anxiety stemming from her family dynamics. The couple's once easy-going rapport began to strain under the weight of unspoken feelings. During a particularly tense moment, after an argument that left them both feeling misunderstood, they reached out to a therapist who encouraged them to create a safe environment for emotional expression.

This pivotal moment revealed to Mia and James that authenticity was not merely about sharing happy moments but articulating pain, fear, and vulnerability. Through the guidance of their therapist, they learned to embrace authenticity by cultivating trust and being open with each other. They began an emotional dialogue that allowed them to address their internal struggles collaboratively, revealing that true connection emerges when partners step beyond superficiality and confront their authentic selves.

Trust forms the foundation of authenticity. It is the assurance that we can share our deepest thoughts and feelings without fear of betrayal or ridicule. The journey of building trust begins with self-awareness; understanding one's feelings and beliefs is essential to communicating them effectively to a partner. Mia realized that she had to confront her anxiety and communicate it to James rather than withdrawing into silence. By doing so, she gifted him the opportunity to support her, gradually weaving a stronger bond of trust.

In conversations that unfolded between them, they discussed their fears of inadequacy, the pressure to succeed, and the weight of their childhood experiences.

Each disclosure was a brick laid in the fragile yet essential structure of trust. James shared his struggles with career setbacks, a topic he had previously avoided for fear of appearing weak. To his surprise, Mia's response was not one of judgment but one filled with empathy and support. This mutual sharing of vulnerabilities paved the way for a connection buoyed by trust and genuine understanding.

Vulnerability, too, is a crucial pillar of authentic relationships. To be vulnerable means to willingly expose oneself to uncertainty and emotional risks. In a society that often glorifies strength and stoicism, the act of being vulnerable can be daunting. Yet, vulnerability is not synonymous with weakness; rather, it is an acknowledgment of our humanity. It offers a powerful means to connect with others at a profound level.

The journey towards vulnerability was no easy feat for Mia and James. Initially, they grappled with discomfort and fear when sharing their authentic selves. James often felt embarrassed about his feelings of inadequacy, while Mia battled the instinct to shield her anxiety. However, as they practiced opening up to each other, they discovered the rewards of vulnerability—the appreciation of their shared humanity, the ability to alleviate personal burdens through mutual support, and the creation of space for emotional intimacy.

As they shared their experiences, James and Mia recognized the strength found in vulnerability. The discussions helped them forge deeper connections not simply through shared laughter but through mutual support during difficult times. Each revelation was a testament to their trust, allowing them to build a relationship grounded in safety. They began to appreciate the beauty in their exposed selves—no longer mere titles as "successful" or "strong," but as individuals grappling with real-life circumstances. This journey illuminated the road toward emotional openness, another cornerstone of building authentic connections.

Emotional openness is the practice of expressing one's feelings and thoughts freely in the relationship. It invites partners to share their dreamscapes, fears, disappointments, and joys, creating an environment where differences are acknowledged and valued, rather than suppressed. The emotional landscape of a relationship thrives when both partners can articulate their needs and desires candidly while feeling assured that their emotions will be received with understanding.

For Mia and James, emotional openness became a regular practice. They designated "check-in" evenings every week, where they would candidly discuss what was weighing on their minds. These sessions opened pathways for discussion that might have otherwise remained dormant. More than just tackling immediate issues, these conversations unearthed underlying desires and aspirations that had been obscured by the daily grind of life.

During one of these intimate evenings, an emotional revelation from Mia shifted the dynamics of their relationship. She confessed that she often felt isolated in her struggles and feared that James could not understand the depth of her anxieties. When James responded with vulnerability—expressing his own feelings of inadequacy and fear of failure—it was as if they crossed an invisible threshold into a deeper realm of understanding. The resultant conversation not only alleviated Mia's sense of isolation but also built a solid foundation of emotional support for James.

Experts in relationships emphasize the importance of fostering emotional openness as a process rather than a one-time event. According to Dr. Laura B. Brown, a clinical psychologist specializing in couple's therapy, cultivating emotional safety requires continuous effort. "Partners need to consistently provide one another with affirmation and validation, especially when emotions are heightened," she states, highlighting that this approach not only consists of listening but actively responding with empathy and understanding.

To illustrate this, consider the story of Alex and Sophia, who faced a moment of crisis when Sophia's mother was hospitalized. Initially, Alex struggled to find the right words to comfort his partner as he felt overwhelmed by the seriousness of the situation. Each attempt at communication felt clumsy and inadequate. However, after realizing that mere words weren't the remedy, he began to lean into emotional openness. By expressing his own fears and vulnerabilities about losing someone he cherished, he was able to create a space for Sophia to voice her tumultuous feelings.

Instead of retreating from the emotional imbalance, they leaned into their authentic selves. Through their raw and honest communication, they learned to share not just in moments of stability but also in fragility. This emotional back-and-forth fostered a sense of solidarity that fortified their bond in ways they had never anticipated.

In establishing a safe space for authenticity, it is critical to encourage open dialogue without judgment. Creating such an environment involves commitment from both partners to actively listen and demonstrate empathy, which can be refined through practice. As Mia and James developed their connection, they learned to ask questions that prompted vulnerability, turning ordinary discussions into opportunities for authentic sharing. Peeking beneath the surface enabled them to explore the complexities of one another's emotions, leading to deeper intimacy.

However, the journey to authenticity is not devoid of challenges. As partners strive for emotional intimacy and openness, they may encounter internal conflicts such as fear of rejection or past experiences that impede their willingness to share fully. Discomfort is an inherent part of the process. Encouraging patience and compassion for oneself and one's partner is paramount. Building authenticity takes time, as partners learn to navigate their emotional topographies together without rushing through feelings.

Adding depth to the narrative, Mia and James sought feedback from their therapist about the obstacles they faced in communicating openly. Gaining insights into their struggles helped them recognize that moments of silence and discomfort were not indicative of failure; rather, they were integral to personal and relational growth. They embraced these moments, viewing them as building blocks toward authenticity.

It's essential to highlight that authenticity also extends beyond conversations. Actions speak volumes in fostering genuine connections. Timely gestures, acts of kindness, and adherence to commitments solidify the authenticity of emotional exchanges. For Mia and James, small acts of love—like preparing a meal after a long day or leaving a note of encouragement—became expressions of their genuine affection for each other, fortifying the words they spoke.

As the foundation of their relationship solidified, Mia and James began to experience a remarkable shift in their connection. Their experiences showcased that authenticity does not equate to a perfect relationship; rather, it involves a willingness to confront fears, embrace vulnerabilities, and ultimately, share the entirety of oneself with a partner. With their newfound framework of trust, vulnerability, and emotional openness, they fostered a connection that transcended the superficiality often prevalent in relationships.

With each hurdle overcome, they unearthed revelations about each other that previously lay dormant. Authenticity allowed them to directly address problems rather than skirt around them, building a reservoir of emotional intimacy that served as a refuge during turbulent times. Their journey underscored the profound potential for deep connection when partners commit to breaking down barriers that inhibit fragile honesty.

As they backpacked through life's unpredictability, Mia and James cultivated a relationship steeped in authenticity—a lasting testament to their commitment to one another. They learned to embrace moments of joy and sorrow as opportunities to delve deeper into their authentic selves.

In fostering authenticity, partners must recognize that they are not merely embarking on an individual journey but mutually navigating a shared path. Creating a culture of authenticity in a relationship requires responsibility, graciousness, and unwavering commitment to creating a space that invites emotional expression. The beauty of authenticity lies in its capacity to illuminate our connections, revealing not only who we are as individuals but who we can become together. Through the elements of trust, vulnerability, and emotional openness, we chase the fundamental truth that authentic connections gradually evolve, rendering life's journey all the more beautiful.

Nurturing Emotional Intimacy

In the tapestry of relationships, emotional intimacy stands as one of the most vibrant threads, weaving partners together through shared experiences, empathy, and deep understanding. It is the invisible cord that connects hearts, allowing individuals to navigate the tumultuous seas of life side by side. Nurturing this intimacy requires deliberate effort, a willingness to engage earnestly, and a commitment to understanding each other on a profound level. As couples aspire to build authentic connections, embracing strategies that enhance emotional bonding can transform their relationships into secure havens of love and trust.

One of the cornerstones of emotional intimacy is active listening. To truly listen is to engage in a dialogue that goes beyond words, encompassing body language, emotional cues, and an open heart. Many couples underestimate the power of this fundamental practice, often distracted by their own thoughts or preoccupations during conversations. Effective listening asks for undivided attention and responsiveness, creating a safe environment for partners to share their innermost feelings.

Consider the story of Maria and James, a couple who struggled with communication. Maria often felt unheard when she shared her concerns about work stress, and James would respond with surface-level advice. The turning point came when they attended a workshop on active listening, where they learned to fully focus on each other's words without interruptions. One evening, as Maria expressed her frustrations, James made a conscious effort to listen without offering immediate solutions. He nodded, maintained eye contact, and used affirming responses. When Maria shared that she felt overwhelmed and needed emotional support rather than problem-solving, James realized how essential it was to simply be present. This small shift in their dynamic fostered a greater sense of closeness, allowing them to understand not just each other's experiences but also the emotions underlying their concerns.

Empathy is another crucial ingredient in the recipe for emotional intimacy. It goes beyond sympathy—where one may feel sorry for a partner's predicament—and invites partners to put themselves in each other's shoes. Through empathy, individuals can grasp the emotional landscape of their partner's experiences, allowing for deeper connections. The essence of empathy lies in validating feelings, acknowledging struggles, and being present with a partner in their moment of need.

Take, for instance, Aaron and Priya, who faced a crisis when Priya lost her job. Initially, Aaron struggled to relate to the intensity of Priya's feelings, having never experienced unemployment himself. However, Aaron made an effort to engage with Priya's emotions by asking open-ended questions about her feelings. He discovered how her job loss affected her self-worth and sense of identity. By responding with compassion, Aaron helped Priya feel seen and understood rather than isolated in her struggle. This emotional connection not only strengthened their bond but also empowered Priya in her journey to recover from the setback.

Shared experiences are also pivotal in nurturing emotional intimacy. The moments that couples create together—whether through adventure, quiet time, or shared goals—form memories that reinforce their connection. Engaging in activities that foster collaboration and interaction can serve as catalysts for bonding, as they create opportunities for vulnerability, laughter, and shared joy.

Jess and Sam exemplify this through their commitment to a weekly date night, where they explore new experiences together—trying new restaurants, attending art classes, or engaging in outdoor activities. During one of their hikes, they encountered a challenging trail. Instead of focusing on the difficulty, they laughed, encouraged each other, and celebrated small victories along the way. This shared experience became a cherished memory for them and reminded them of their teamwork and resilience as a couple. The laughter and camaraderie during their hike deepened their sense of connection, showing them that emotional intimacy thrives not only in words but also in moments of togetherness.

Another powerful strategy for fostering emotional intimacy is the practice of gratitude. Expressing appreciation for one another creates a positive reinforcement loop, enhancing emotional bonds and fostering a deeper sense of security. Acts of gratitude—whether in small gestures or heartfelt expressions—serve to remind partners of their value in each other's lives.

When Maria began to regularly express gratitude for the little things James did, such as making her coffee in the morning or supporting her during busy days, it triggered a shift in their relationship dynamic. James felt more appreciated and became increasingly attuned to Maria's needs as well. This cycle of appreciation prompted both to seek ways to express love and affection, enriching their emotional intimacy.

To enhance emotional intimacy further, couples can establish rituals of connection. These are specific practices or routines that create opportunities for intimacy in everyday life. Simple practices, such as sharing a morning coffee, having a nightly debrief about the day, or holding hands while watching a movie, can be effective at fostering connection and deepening understanding over time.

Sophia and Alex, married for five years, noticed that their busy schedules often left little room for intimacy. They decided to create a nightly ritual where they would spend 15 minutes before bed to share highlights of their day. This practice not only allowed them to unwind together but also prompted deeper conversations about their dreams, worries, and aspirations. It became a sacred space where they felt safe to explore each other's thoughts, solidifying their emotional bond.

Communication is the lifeblood of emotional

intimacy. Open, honest conversations build trust and alleviate misunderstandings. Couples should prioritize creating a space where both can express their feelings without fear of judgment. This means being vulnerable and sharing fears, dreams, and insecurities, as exposing these facets of oneself fosters deep connections.

Carl and Jenna often practiced sharing their thoughts and feelings on alternate nights, known as "Vulnerability Wednesdays." During these dedicated sessions, they would take turns discussing something personal that they had yet to share. One Wednesday, Carl revealed his insecurities about his career, expressing fear that he was not living up to potential expectations. Jenna's supportive response reassured him; this practice allowed both to share their deepest feelings regularly, reinforcing their emotional connection.

Physical affection also plays a vital role in enhancing emotional intimacy. Touch can communicate love and affection in ways that words sometimes cannot. Simple acts like holding hands, hugging, or cuddling can strengthen the emotional bond and create a sense of safety and warmth between partners.

After a long day, Rachel and Paul made it a point to spend at least 10 minutes cuddling on the couch, simply being present with one another. This practice helped them transition from their hectic days, reminding them of their love and commitment. Rachel shared that the soothing rhythm of their cuddling became a grounding practice that signified the end of a workday and the start of devoted time together.

Creating an atmosphere of safety and trust is essential for cultivating emotional intimacy. Couples should strive to build a space where both partners feel free to express their thoughts, emotions, and vulnerabilities without fear of being criticized or dismissed. When partners feel safe in their relationship, they are more willing to share their true selves, fostering connection and understanding.

Emotional intimacy can often be tested by external stressors—financial pressures, familial obligations, or professional obligations. Couples who can weather these storms together often emerge stronger and more closely bonded. During challenging times, the ability to lean on each other for emotional support becomes vital.

During a particularly challenging phase, when Olivia lost a family member, her partner Noah showed up for her in a way that reaffirmed their emotional intimacy. Instead of shying away from discussing Olivia's loss, Noah willingly provided a listening ear and comforted her, sometimes just by holding her hand through the tough days. Their shared grief brought them closer, as they learned to navigate the complexities of loss together, reinforcing their connection through compassion and emotional support.

Emotionally charged conversations can sometimes lead to disagreements and misunderstandings. It is crucial for couples to learn and practice conflict resolution strategies that foster intimacy rather than drive them apart. By approaching conflicts with curiosity and an open heart, partners can transform disagreements into opportunities for growth.

Lisa and Tom often struggled with conflict

resolution, but after attending a couple's retreat, they learned to engage in "compassionate communication." They began using "I" statements rather than "you" statements, focusing on expressing personal feelings without casting blame. For example, instead of saying "You never listen to me," Lisa would express, "I feel unheard when you look at your phone during our conversations." This approach led to deeper discussions about each other's needs, ultimately enhancing their emotional intimacy.

A crucial aspect of nurturing emotional intimacy is embracing vulnerability. Trust is built upon the willingness to be seen and accepted wholly, flaws and all. By allowing each other to witness their imperfections, couples foster deeper connections and create an environment where vulnerability feels safe.

Jake and Sandra had long struggled with intimacy until they each decided to dive deeper into their emotional worlds. During one profound conversation, Jake openly shared his struggles with anxiety, describing how it impacted his behavior and interactions. Sandra listened, offered reassurance, and shared her own struggles with self-doubt. By showing vulnerability, they transcended previous barriers, both feeling lighter and more connected.

It's essential to recognize that nurturing emotional intimacy is an ongoing process. As life evolves, so do the needs and dynamics within relationships. Couples must be willing to adapt, learn, and reinvest in their emotional connection continually. Engaging with workshops, reading relationship-oriented literature, or seeking professional guidance can provide couples with fresh perspectives and tools to enhance their emotional bonds.

Lastly, couples should remind themselves that emotional intimacy is not a destination but a journey—one that requires patience, commitment, and a genuine desire to nurture connection. By actively participating in the process, partners can deepen their connections and create fulfilling, lasting relationships.

As we reflect on the myriad ways to foster emotional intimacy, it becomes evident that the journey requires intention and effort. By embracing active listening, practicing empathy, sharing experiences, and maintaining open communication, couples can create a robust foundation for emotional growth. Ultimately, it is the small, consistent actions that pave the way for deeper connections, allowing love to flourish in its most authentic form. In a world where convenience often overshadows authenticity, those who prioritize emotional intimacy will find themselves stepping into a realm of genuine partnership, capable not only of surmounting obstacles together but of relishing the beauty of shared love and connection.

The Role of Shared Values

Shared values serve as the bedrock upon which authentic relationships are built. When two partners align on fundamental beliefs and goals, they create a framework that fosters understanding, trust, and mutual respect. This alignment forms the foundation from which love can grow, paving the way for a connection that transcends fleeting emotions or superficial attractions. Consequently, navigating the complexities of a relationship becomes more manageable when both partners are grounded in shared values, as it enables them to tackle challenges and differences with a united front.

To delve deeper into the significance of shared values, we turn to the insights offered by couples who have confronted the realities of differing beliefs yet found ways to navigate these essential aspects of their relationships. Their stories illuminate the path for others who may be facing similar struggles, offering hope and guidance on how to engage in meaningful discussions about values.

One couple we spoke with, Sarah and Jake, epitomizes the journey of aligning values within a relationship. They initially attracted each other through their shared interests; however, as their relationship deepened, they discovered fundamental differences in their values that tested their bond. Sarah values career ambition and personal growth, believing that striving for success is crucial for fulfillment. Conversely, Jake's values center around family and community, where meaningful connections and shared experiences reign supreme.

At first, these differences created friction, as Sarah felt Jake's emphasis on family commitments was a hindrance to her professional aspirations. Meanwhile, Jake grappled with feeling neglected and unimportant when Sarah prioritized her work commitments over family gatherings. The couple realized that without open discussions about their core values, they risked drifting apart. They decided to sit down and openly explore each other's beliefs, goals, and priorities, setting aside their defensiveness and striving to understand one another.

Through these discussions, Sarah began to appreciate the significance Jake placed on familial ties; she realized that supporting one another's aspirations could fortify their relationship rather than threaten it. Jake, in turn, came to understand that Sarah's ambitions were not a rejection of their shared life but an extension of it. He recognized that her success could create opportunities for the family they were building. This revelation shifted their dynamic, as they articulated how their differing values could coexist and complement one another rather than colliding.

Such open discussions revealed the interconnectedness of their dreams, reinforcing their commitment to each other and their shared future. By aligning on key values—such as the importance of open communication, respect for ambitions, and a commitment to family—they established a mutually supportive environment, allowing both partners to thrive as individuals while remaining connected as a couple. This intentional effort to explore and articulate their values ultimately reinforced their bond, illuminating the path to authentic connection.

Another couple, Chandra and Amir, was faced with an equally challenging situation. Both had grown up in different cultural backgrounds, which informed their perspectives on marriage, religion, and child-rearing. In their early days together, they were swept away by the romance and excitement of their relationship. However, as discussions about marriage and starting a family emerged, they encountered stark contrasts in their values that required thoughtful navigation.

Chandra, who grew up in a secular household that emphasized personal freedoms and individual choices, found it difficult to understand Amir's strong ties to his cultural and religious background, which prioritized community traditions and collective values. Amir, raised with a deep sense of belonging within his culturally rich family, struggled with the idea of diverging from those traditions in favor of more liberal approaches to family life that Chandra advocated.

Recognizing the potential impact of these differing values on their future, Chandra and Amir engaged in candid dialogues, not only about what values mattered to each of them but also about why those values held significance in their lives. They began exploring questions such as, "What does family mean to us?" "How do we view commitment?" and "What ideals do we wish to impart to our future children?" This exploration helped them uncover the underlying motivations behind their beliefs, opening windows of empathy and understanding.

Through their conversations, Chandra recognized that Amir's attachment to his cultural heritage stemmed from a desire to honor his family's legacy and provide a sense of belonging for future generations. Amir, in turn, grasped that Chandra's emphasis on personal freedom wasn't a rejection of family values but rather an expression of individual growth that could lead to enriching experiences for both of them. This mutual understanding laid the groundwork for compromise, as they collectively crafted a vision for their married life that acknowledged and embraced both cultural perspectives.

As they charted their course, they established essential shared values: respect for traditions alongside a commitment to modern ideals, the importance of family bonding while fostering individual identities, and the recognition that love meant honoring and celebrating their differences rather than allowing them to be barriers. Chandra and Amir's ability to align their values not only solidified their partnership but also inspired them to create a unique entity—a blended family dynamic that embraced both their cultural heritages.

In contrast to the stories of Sarah and Jake, and Chandra and Amir, other couples may find themselves caught in the turmoil of undiscussed values, leading to challenges that feel insurmountable. One such couple, Mark and Lisa, began their relationship with an intense, passionate romance, fueled by a powerful physical attraction and shared hobbies. They were ecstatic and believed their connection was invincible.

However, they later confronted stark differences in their fundamental belief systems when discussions of finances and future aspirations arose. Mark, having grown up in a family that operated on the principle of frugality and saving, believed in careful financial planning and stability. On the other hand, Lisa valued spontaneity and experiences, often prioritizing travel and adventure over long-term savings.

Initially, their conversations about how to manage their finances devolved into arguments, as both felt misunderstood and dismissed. Lisa accused Mark of being overly anxious and restrictive, while Mark viewed Lisa's lifestyle as reckless and irresponsible. Instead of fanning the flames of their differences, they sought the guidance of a relationship therapist to navigate the discord stemming from their differing values.

Through guided conversations with the therapist, they began to unpack their beliefs and the emotions attached to them. They explored what money represented for each of them—security, freedom, opportunity, and enjoyment. Clarifying the values behind their beliefs allowed them to replace accusations with curiosity and judgement with understanding.

Ultimately, they recognized that both perspectives could coexist. They collaborated on creating a budget that allowed for a reasonable allocation of funds—some dedicated toward experiences Lisa valued while also prioritizing security and savings that Mark deemed essential. By embracing their shared values—of commitment, support, and mutual respect—they were able to forge a common path that synthesized their differing beliefs.

These narratives assert the importance of unearthing and articulating shared values as a means of enriching relationships. However, beyond mere discussion, the cultivation of shared values requires action. Establishing and nurturing shared values emanates from a commitment to regularly engage in conversations about beliefs, aspirations, and challenges. Couples must create opportunities to discuss not only their current values but also their evolving beliefs as their lives transpire.

Questions that elicit deep reflection can facilitate fruitful conversations. Couples might consider engaging in dialogues surrounding themes such as:

- What values do you hold most dearly, and how have they been shaped by your upbringing and

experiences?
- How do we envision our ideal relationship as shaped by our values?
- What core values can we establish together to guide our decisions, particularly in the face of challenges?
- In what ways can we honor each other's individual values while fostering our connection?

While reframing the context of value discussions is essential, practical exercises can further solidify shared beliefs. Couples may choose to engage in activities such as creating a shared vision board or exploring community service projects that resonate with their values. These experiences can anchor their beliefs in tangible realities, reinforcing their commitment to fostering an environment that honors both their individual identities and collective aspirations.

The connection between values, love, and commitment is a profound one. When partners genuinely align on values, they cultivate a nurturing space where love can intertwine and flourish, anchored in mutual understanding and acceptance. Values frame how partners navigate obstacles and face life's uncertainties together, creating a sense of unified purpose that extends beyond the couple, embracing their shared life, family, and community.

As readers reflect on their own relationships, it is vital to assess whether their values truly align with those of their partners. Are there core beliefs that remain unarticulated or unexamined? Are partners truly engaging in discussions about their values and aspirations, or are they passively accepting them as they surface in the relationship? Such reflections can awaken a desire for deeper connection and growth, propelling couples toward a more authentic partnership.

Moreover, the interdependence of values introduces the critical understanding that commitment transcends mere romantic love; it invokes the idea of nurturing a partnership anchored in shared principles. As relationships evolve, partners may find new dimensions of enrichment when based on a foundation of aligned values. Equipped with clear communication and genuine understanding, partners foster a dynamic that embraces growth, recognizes differences, and weaves them into the fabric of a loving, lasting connection.

The pursuit of authentic love necessitates an unwavering commitment to nurturing values that resonate deeply within each partner while cherishing and honoring what makes each individual unique. In this context, moving beyond superficial offerings enables partners to connect authentically and cultivate resilient relationships built on the tenets of understanding and shared purpose.

As this subchapter illustrates, the significance of shared values cannot be overstated when considering the essence of love, authenticity, and commitment in relationships. By fostering open dialogue and conscious reflections, partners can align their values, creating a harmonious environment that bolsters their emotional intimacy and connection. Ultimately, it is through shared values that couples can thrive, transcending individual aspirations to embrace a shared destiny—a journey rooted in love, commitment, and authentic connection.

The Role of Communication

Effective Communication Strategies

In the intricate dance of relationships, communication serves as the music that guides us. The rhythms of our conversations can either pulse with harmony or clash with dissonance, shaping the trajectory of our partnerships. As we navigate the complexities of marriage, it becomes imperative to cultivate a repertoire of effective communication strategies that foster open dialogue and understanding. This subchapter aims to equip readers with critical skills—active listening, assertive expression, and nonverbal communication—providing practical tools that enhance interactions and create emotional safety within partnerships.

At the heart of effective communication lies active listening—a practice that transcends mere hearing to foster genuine understanding. Active listening involves fully engaging with our partners' words, emotions, and intentions. It requires a delicate balance of attentiveness that lets our partners feel seen and heard. When we practice active listening, we offer our partners the greatest gift: the validation of their feelings and thoughts. This act not only fosters intimacy but also establishes a foundation of trust and respect that is vital for any healthy relationship.

Consider the story of Maria and Tom, a couple who struggled with feeling disconnected over the years. Frequently, they found themselves in cycles of disagreement, with each partner frustrated that the other never seemed to understand their perspective. During a pivotal moment in their relationship, they decided to commit to practicing active listening. They set aside time each week for a "listening hour," during which they would take turns sharing their thoughts without interruptions.

In their first session, Maria spoke about her frustrations at work, expressing feelings of inadequacy and stress. Rather than jumping in with solutions or counter-arguments, Tom practiced active listening. He made eye contact, nodded understandingly, and responded with reflective statements such as, "It sounds like you're feeling overwhelmed and unappreciated." By mirroring her feelings back to her, he offered her the emotional validation she craved. Maria felt a burden lifting, and for the first time in a long while, she sensed that Tom truly understood her experiences.

Tom's journey with active listening allowed him to appreciate Maria's emotional landscape. By feeling acknowledged, Maria had the space to process her feelings without the pressure of finding immediate solutions. The couple reported that this simple adjustment to their communication strategy transformed their arguments into productive discussions, where each partner felt valued and understood. This approach minimized misunderstandings and enabled them to confront issues more collaboratively rather than combatively.

Alongside active listening, assertive expression plays a critical role in effective communication. Assertiveness empowers individuals to express their thoughts, feelings, and needs openly and respectfully, fostering an atmosphere of honesty. When partners learn to articulate their feelings assertively, they reduce the need for passive-aggressive behavior, which often breeds resentment. Importantly, assertive communication creates a platform for constructive dialogue where both partners feel comfortable sharing their truths.

In the case of Jordan and Leah, assertiveness became pivotal in addressing long-standing tensions regarding household responsibilities. Leah often felt overwhelmed by the chores, believing Jordan was indifferent to their shared commitments. When Leah initially voiced her frustrations, her approach was indirect and laced with negativity, leading to defensiveness from Jordan. However, after engaging in a couple's workshop focused on communication, Leah learned the value of assertive expression.

The next time household responsibilities became a topic of discussion, Leah adopted a direct approach. "Jordan, I need to talk to you about how we manage our chores. I've been feeling stressed and overwhelmed, and I genuinely need your support." This line not only expressed her feelings but also clarified her need for assistance, establishing a fertile ground for collaboration rather than conflict.

Jordan felt a shift occurring; rather than feeling attacked or criticized, he sensed openness and vulnerability from Leah. He was more inclined to respond positively, "I didn't realize you were feeling this way. How can we work together to balance the chores more effectively?" Leah's assertive expression cultivated a space for both partners to brainstorm solutions collectively, enhancing their ability to work as a team rather than adversaries.

While verbal communication significantly enhances connections, nonverbal communication is equally vital. The words we choose are often supplemented—or contradicted—by our body language, tone of voice, and facial expressions. In fact, studies suggest that nonverbal cues constitute as much as 93% of communication. Thus, being attuned to nonverbal signals can profoundly impact a couple's interaction.

For example, consider Ella and Marcus, who often found themselves arguing during discussions about finances. Despite their words' intentions, Ella's crossed arms and furrowed brow sent a message of defensiveness and frustration, clouding the conversation. Meanwhile, when Marcus kept his body turned away or stared at his phone, Ella felt dismissed. Realizing that nonverbal communication hampered their ability to connect, they decided to focus on enhancing their nonverbal cues.

During their discussions, they consciously practiced maintaining open body language—turning to one another, maintaining eye contact, and even leaning slightly forward to signal interest and engagement. They also adjusted their tone to match the gravity of their conversations. By fostering an environment where their body language aligned with their words, they found it easier to navigate sensitive topics without escalating tensions further. Ella described how much more welcome and appreciated she felt when Marcus's body language mirrored his verbal commitment to be present and receptive.

Creating a safe space for open discussions is another linchpin in effective communication. Emotional safety encourages vulnerability and honesty among partners, allowing them to express their feelings without fear of judgment or backlash. 'The Advocate' suggests several tips for cultivating such a space within relationships.

First, establishing ground rules for discussions can greatly enhance emotional safety. Couples can agree to seek understanding before responding, refrain from personal attacks, and use "I" statements to express their feelings and experiences. For example, using "I feel neglected when we don't spend time together on weekends" instead of "You never want to do anything with me" changes the focus from blame to personal feelings.

Additionally, practicing empathy during discussions builds emotional safety. When one partner shares their feelings, the other should take the time to validate those feelings even if they don't fully agree. Emphasizing empathy reinforces the idea that all emotions are legitimate; thus no partner has to feel isolated in their experiences. "I can understand how that might feel overwhelming" or "It sounds like you're dealing with a lot right now" can be powerful empathetic phrases that foster connection.

It is also crucial to establish routines or rituals that promote open dialogue in a low-pressure context. Perhaps a designated "check-in" at the end of each week provides partners a structured time to share how they're feeling about their relationship, their needs, or any concerns they may have. This anticipated moment becomes a psychological safety net, diminishing the dread of potentially contentious conversations.

Building emotional safety requires dedication and practice from both partners, leading to deeper emotional intimacy over time. For instance, Sophie and Alex created a weekly ritual called "Sunday debriefs" where they dedicated time to reflect on their week, express grievances, and celebrate wins. Because they cultivated a consistent space free from distractions, they found it easier to express their genuine feelings, minimizing conflict and maximizing understanding.

To illustrate the real-life applications of these communication strategies, let us return to Maria and Tom. While embracing active listening and assertive expression, they also invested time in understanding the nuances of nonverbal communication. They committed to fostering an emotionally safe environment where both could share their vulnerabilities without hesitation.

One evening, Maria decided to approach a sensitive topic regarding the potential move to a new city for job opportunities. Instead of presenting this news as a command or demand, she embraced the principles of assertive communication. "Tom, I want to talk about the possibility of relocating for my job. I'm both excited and anxious about it, and I'd love to know how you feel about this change." By inviting Tom into the conversation while openly sharing her emotions, Maria established an atmosphere conducive to productive dialogue.

As the conversation unfolded, Tom realized this subject carried significant weight for both of them. He used active listening to echo back Maria's feelings: "It sounds like this opportunity could bring both excitement and anxiety for you. Moving is a big change for us." As Maria felt heard and understood, she felt safe to express her fears about uprooting their lives. Eventually, this discussion led them to brainstorm potential agreements that could alleviate their concerns.

Tom reflected on the power of nonverbal signals during this conversation. He made sure to maintain eye contact and nodding, signaling his attentiveness. Rather than shutting down the conversation with a distant stance, he adopted open body language, which reinforced the emotional safety Maria needed to articulate her feelings.

However, even in a harmonious setting, misunderstandings can still arise. During one session, Tom unintentionally diverted the conversation by sharing his doubts about the move, which made Maria feel as though her concerns were disregarded. Rather than allowing this moment to spiral into an argument, Maria remembered their commitment to honesty and emotional safety. She calmly expressed, "I appreciate your perspective, but it feels like my feelings about moving are getting overshadowed. Can we focus on my concerns for a moment?"

This moment of assertive expression redirected their dialogue constructively; Tom realized the importance of holding space for Maria's emotions rather than shifting the focus to his own. The couple emerged from that difficult conversation more equipped to navigate potential challenges together.

These moments illuminate the profound impact effective communication can have on the quality and longevity of a relationship. As partners learn to engage with one another authentically, they form a shared understanding that enables them to tackle challenges collaboratively. Remember that the journey toward effective communication is not linear; it requires commitment, patience, and practice.

As the narrative of Maria and Tom illustrates, successful communication is not the absence of conflict but rather the ability to navigate it compassionately and openly. Active listening, assertive expression, and awareness of nonverbal cues equip couples with the tools to foster emotional safety, encouraging mutual understanding. When partners apply these strategies consistently, they cultivate a deeper emotional bond, enriching their relationship and transforming it into a safe haven for both love and growth.

Ultimately, fostering an environment of open dialogue may involve trial and error—embracing lessons learned along the way. It invites couples to reflect regularly on their communication habits and challenges, creating awareness around potential barriers. Empowered by knowledge and practiced strategies, individuals can forge deeper connections that transcend mere communication, paving the way for authentic intimacy and lasting love. In navigating the intricacies of partnership, these strategies will serve as guiding lights, illuminating the path toward a fulfilling relationship built on trust, respect, and genuine connection.

Overcoming Communication Barriers

In the intricate tapestry of relationships, communication serves as the vital thread that connects partners, shaping the understanding and intimacy between them. However, when this thread frays or becomes entangled in common barriers, the potential for connection can diminish significantly. Couples often find themselves caught in cycles of defensiveness, criticism, and avoidance, which can obstruct the open dialogue necessary for relationship growth.

Consider the story of Sarah and Mark, a couple married for five years. They once felt deeply connected, but over time, they began to experience a growing distance. Their conversations, once flowing easily, had become fraught with tension. Mark often felt criticized in discussions about household responsibilities, while Sarah perceived his responses as defensive and dismissive. This cycle led to frequent misunderstandings and, ultimately, feelings of resentment.

As their relationship stagnated, they recognized their communication patterns were at the heart of their troubles. They learned that the first step toward improvement was acknowledging the barriers that had taken root in their interactions.

Defensiveness is one of the most common and detrimental barriers to effective communication. It often arises in response to perceived attacks, whether verbal or non-verbal. For Mark, Sarah's feedback about a messy kitchen felt like criticism rather than an invitation to collaborate. His instinctive defensiveness triggered a defensive posture, dampening Sarah's intentions. This vicious cycle often exacerbates tensions, making both parties feel unheard and unvalued.

To counter defensiveness, couples can practice the art of non-defensive listening. This involves actively engaging with what the other person is saying, without immediately resorting to a defensive reaction. Acknowledging their partner's feelings—even if one does not agree with their perspective—can create a more inviting atmosphere for dialogue. Mark began to realize that instead of preparing his rebuttal when Sarah brought up concerns, he could listen and validate her feelings first. By doing this, he began to unwind the tension between them and re-establish a sense of connection.

Criticism, another significant barrier, has a way of eroding the foundation of trust and respect in relationships. It's easy for one partner to frame their feedback in terms of the other's character rather than their behaviors. Sarah often used phrases like, "You never help around the house," which inadvertently painted Mark as lazy and uninvolved rather than addressing the specific behavior that was bothering her. The distinction between a helpful critique of one's actions—"It feels overwhelming when I'm doing all the chores by myself"—and outright criticism can be subtle yet crucial.

To navigate criticism effectively, couples can adopt a technique known as "I-statements." These allow individuals to express their feelings regarding certain behaviors without attributing blame. For instance, Sarah could instead say, "I feel stressed when I see the laundry piling up, and I would really appreciate your help." This not only communicates her feelings but also invites Mark to engage positively.

Then there's the barrier of avoidance, which can manifest in silence, withdrawal, or even passive-aggressiveness. Avoidance often arises when individuals fear conflict or have learned that addressing certain topics leads to pain or frustration. In the case of Sarah and Mark, they would frequently avoid discussing finances, fearing it would lead to arguments over spending and budgeting. This avoidance only served to deepen their divide, as unaddressed issues continued to fester beneath the surface.

To combat avoidance, couples must cultivate an environment of safety where open discussions can occur without fear of judgment or escalation. This might entail setting aside specific times to talk about challenging topics, ensuring both partners are in a calm frame of mind. They could also agree to approach such discussions with an open heart, aiming for understanding rather than winning an argument.

As Sarah and Mark explored these barriers, they began to understand their emotional dynamics and how these patterns influenced their communication. They started holding weekly check-ins, providing a structured space where they could express frustrations and celebrate successes without the weight of daily stressors. These sessions became a lifeline for their relationship, allowing them to discuss financial concerns, household responsibilities, and more—transforming potential points of conflict into opportunities for growth.

At the heart of overcoming these communication barriers is the profound realization that vulnerability and empathy are essential. When couples allow themselves to be vulnerable, they not only share their fears and concerns but also extend trust to their partners. This mutual openness nurtures emotional intimacy, creating a safe haven for explorative communication.

To illustrate this necessity, take the story of Jane and Tom. They had been together for eight years, yet they were trapped in a constant pattern of frustration. Tom often felt that Jane undervalued his opinions during discussions. Jane, on the other hand, struggled with expressing her thoughts out of fear that Tom would dismiss them. Their communication became a series of missed opportunities and misunderstandings.

Recognizing their emotional impasse, they decided to embark on a journey of vulnerability. They each wrote down their fears about being heard and understood in their relationship, discovering both similarities and differences in their experiences. By sharing these written reflections in a calm and safe setting, they opened the door to deeper conversations.

During this process, they learned to practice the skills of empathy and understanding. Tom listened to Jane's concerns about feeling undervalued and, in return, opened up about his fears of inadequacy. This two-way communication ultimately strengthened their connection, reinforcing their love and commitment to one another.

As they progressed, Jane and Tom cultivated specific strategies to build empathy into their daily interactions. They committed to "mirroring" each other's feelings— echoing back what they heard to ensure comprehension. For instance, if Jane expressed concern about household chores, Tom would respond, "I hear you saying you feel overwhelmed, and it sounds important for us to work together on this."

This technique not only clarified intentions but also reinforced that both partners were heard and understood. It transformed complaints into collaborative strategies aimed at problem-solving, establishing a sense of partnership rather than opposition.

In the realm of communication, timing is also an essential factor. The moments chosen for discussions can significantly affect their outcomes. Engaging in potentially confrontational conversations during high-stress moments—such as when one partner is preoccupied with a difficult day at work—can elevate tensions. To mitigate this, couples can benefit from a technique known as "time-out," where either partner can pause a discussion if emotions run high. By agreeing on a set time to revisit the subject, they grant each other space for processing emotions without negating the necessity of the conversation.

Moreover, utilizing humor can serve as a bridge across communication gaps. While sensitive topics often warrant serious discussions, humor—when appropriate—can diffuse tension and create a more relaxed atmosphere. When Jane and Tom faced disagreements, they learned to incorporate lightheartedness, employing gentle teasing or playful banter to lighten the mood and foster a sense of camaraderie.

It's important to note that overcoming communication barriers isn't an easy or linear process. Sarah, Mark, Jane, and Tom all faced setbacks and challenging conversations, moments that required relentless patience and commitment. They learned that maintaining effective communication requires continuous effort and awareness. The role of communication is not merely about exchanging words; it encompasses the cultivation of a foundation of trust, understanding, and emotional intimacy.

In exploring the emotional layers of effective communication, it becomes clear that individuals must first understand their internal dialogues before engaging in their partner's perspectives. Recognizing and addressing one's own emotional triggers can intricately shape the dynamics of conversations, either paving the way for constructive discourse or leading to unintended conflict.

Each couple must navigate the intricate web of their unique histories, fears, and vulnerabilities while engaging in dialogue. As partners work through their communication barriers, they will inevitably confront their own histories and emotional legacies. With patience and intention, couples can forge pathways to healthier communication, enhancing understanding and intimacy in their relationships.

Ultimately, the journey toward effective communication is a shared endeavor. Acknowledging barriers, fostering vulnerability, and practicing empathy is both a challenge and a labor of love. The stories of couples who have successfully navigated these barriers remind us that the path to connection demands courage, intentionality, and unwavering commitment to one another. By embracing the complexities of communication, partners can cultivate deeply rooted relationships founded on understanding, compassion, and, above all, love.

The Transformative Power of Dialogue

In the intricate landscape of relationships, open communication often acts as the lifeblood that nourishes connection. It is through dialogue that couples share their inner worlds, navigate difficulties, and reaffirm their commitment to one another. While many couples may start their journey with what seems like a natural rapport, it's not uncommon for misunderstandings and unresolved conflicts to arise as the relationship evolves. The transformative power of dialogue becomes paramount in these moments, offering a pathway through conflict, disconnection, and even resentment. As we explore the stories of couples who have bravely engaged in honest conversations, we will highlight how these dialogues not only salvaged their love but often led to greater intimacy and understanding than they had previously known.

Consider the story of Emma and Jake, a couple who had been married for seven years. To the outside world, they appeared to be the perfect couple. They enjoyed a comfortable lifestyle, shared hobbies, and spent time with friends and family. Yet beneath the surface, both Emma and Jake felt a growing distance. They stopped sharing their feelings, opting instead for surface conversations that did little to address the underlying tension brewing in their home. Emma yearned for emotional connection, while Jake felt overwhelmed by work stress and withdrew further into his shell, leading them into a silent spiral of discontent.

One evening, after another mundane day spent in silence, Emma decided to confront the problem directly. She prepared herself mentally and chose a calm moment to express her feelings of loneliness and disappointment. Sitting across from Jake, she took a deep breath and said, "I feel like we've been missing each other lately. I miss the emotional connection we used to have." To her surprise, Jake didn't respond defensively. Instead, he listened. As Emma poured out her heart, admitting her fears and frustrations, Jake felt a wave of relief wash over him. No longer bound by the weight of unspoken words, he found himself able to share his own struggles—that the stress of work had made him retreat, but deep down, he yearned to rekindle their bond.

The result of this honest dialogue was monumental. That night marked the turning point in their relationship. By simply choosing to communicate openly about their feelings, Emma and Jake began to rediscover each other. They established a routine of 'check-in' conversations every Thursday evening, a dedicated time where they explored not only the highs and lows of their week but also their aspirations, fears, and desires. By giving voice to their inner thoughts, they found a new depth of intimacy, realizing that they were not alone in their struggles but partners navigating life together.

Their story illuminates a core tenet about communication: open dialogue fosters vulnerability, and vulnerability builds trust. When each partner feels safe to share their thoughts without fear of judgment or invalidation, a deeper emotional connection forms. This is not merely an isolated incident but a fundamental truth that resonates with many couples. Research in relationship psychology consistently supports the notion that communication is linked to greater relationship satisfaction. Couples who engage in regular discussions about their needs, desires, and conflicts are better equipped to handle the inevitable challenges that arise.

A similar narrative unfolds with Maria and Tom, who faced a very different challenge. After ten years of marriage, they discovered that they had differing views on parenting. Maria loved being hands-on with their children, always engaging in play and educational activities, while Tom preferred to focus on providing for the family financially and occasionally joining in family activities without taking the helm. Initially, this disparity led to frustration on both sides, with Maria feeling that Tom was disengaged and Tom feeling overwhelmed by the responsibilities he believed he had to shoulder alone.

At first, they attempted to address these concerns indirectly. Maria would drop hints about needing more support, while Tom would make vague promises to be more involved. However, it wasn't until a significant disagreement over their son's schooling policy forced them to confront the underlying emotions that they genuinely began to communicate.

In the heat of the moment, rather than resort to blame and defensiveness, Maria suggested they sit down and openly discuss their feelings regarding their child's education and upbringing. They agreed to meet after putting the kids to bed, and as they sat across from each other on their couch, something shifted. Rather than point fingers at one another, they sought to understand the motivations behind each other's perspectives. Maria expressed how much she valued presence and involvement in her children's lives, which came from her own upbringing where both her parents were actively engaged. For Tom, it was about providing stability; he had grown up with a single parent who worked multiple jobs and wasn't always present, which made him yearn to create a different life for his family.

Through this candid dialogue, they uncovered not only their differing views but the deep-seated fears and baggage each carried from their childhood. As they listened and affirmed each other's experiences, they transformed frustration into mutual understanding. This dialogue didn't resolve all their differences overnight, but it set the foundation for collaborative parenting discussions. From that point on, Maria and Tom began to create compromises—Tom committed to taking a more active role in daily activities, while Maria recognized the importance of acknowledging Tom's financial efforts.

Maria and Tom's willingness to communicate openly resulted in a newfound respect and appreciation for each other as partners and co-parents. They actively adopted dialogue as a tool, setting regular family meetings to address potential issues and ensure they remained aligned in their parenting journey, strengthening their emotional connection in the process.

These narratives reveal a profound truth: effective dialogue transforms conflict into an opportunity for growth. Communication is not merely about exchanging words; it encompasses active listening, empathy, and the willingness to be vulnerable. Many couples steer clear of genuine conversations over fears of conflict, believing silence can prevent discord. However, as the stories of Emma, Jake, Maria, and Tom illustrate, avoiding difficult discussions often leads to a buildup of resentment, and disconnection becomes inevitable.

In addition to vulnerability and understanding, open dialogue can significantly enhance emotional intimacy. Consider the case of Lisa and Mark, who had been married for fifteen years but found themselves drifting apart after their children left for college. With their identified roles as parents no longer front and center, they were confronted with an unsettling reality: they no longer recognized each other as a couple. To re-establish their bond, they decided to embark on a weekly date night, but Lisa quickly realized that they avoided discussing any core topics during these outings. Instead of enjoying each other's company, they were caught in nostalgia, recounting the past without addressing their current sentiments and aspirations.

Recognizing this pattern, Lisa proposed a "communication jar"—a jar filled with prompts or questions they could draw upon during their date nights. This gamified approach invited meaningful dialogue while reducing the pressure of a one-on-one conversation. Through trial and error, they learned to navigate topics that elicited deeper introspection, spanning from their fears about life post-retirement to redefining their roles and identities as a couple.

One evening, Mark drew the prompt: "What do you want to be remembered for?" This question opened up an avenue for vulnerability unlike anything they'd shared in years. As they delved into their hopes and fears for the future, Mark revealed his long-held desire to travel the world, pursuing photography—something he had shelved during their busy parenting years. Lisa, in turn, unearthed her dream of writing a book about their family's journey.

This conversation not only reignited their long-buried dreams but also fortified their emotional bonds. They began to envision their future together anew, which created a sense of excitement rather than loss. Their experience highlights how engaging in purposeful dialogue can redefine relationships that have entered a stagnation phase, reigniting passion and commitment.

The undercurrents of these stories serve as fundamental lessons on the importance of prioritizing communication in relationships. The emotional intimacy cultivated through open dialogues not only resolves conflict but also strengthens the very fabric of love. As couples navigate the myriad challenges life throws their way, it is vital to recognize that investing in communication is crucial for fostering connection and understanding.

Prioritizing dialogue can bring immense benefits to relationships. To make strides in this area, couples should first create emotional safety. Establishing a safe space for discussions is an essential step before delving into more profound topics. This often involves setting ground rules for discussions that promote respect and openness. Couples might agree on the importance of listening without interrupting, ensuring that both partners feel valued in their opinions, even when perspectives differ.

Additionally, utilizing specific communication strategies can help facilitate dialogue. Active listening—where one partner reflects back and validates the feelings of the other—can help low-tension discussions snowball into deeper, more meaningful exchanges. Using "I" statements, such as "I feel overwhelmed when..." rather than "You never..." can prevent feelings of blame, transforming the way partners discuss their feelings.

Couples should also adopt regular check-ins in their relationship, where they create intentional opportunities for dialogue. This could be a weekly coffee date or a nightly ritual of sharing highlights and challenges of the day. By normalizing open conversations, couples can tackle issues before they escalate and keep the lines of communication open.

Ultimately, the narrative of couples like Emma and Jake, Maria and Tom, and Lisa and Mark reinforces a vital truth: the transformative power of dialogue is foundational to lasting love and commitment. In an increasingly fast-paced world where distractions abound, prioritizing communication becomes an act of love in itself—an invitation to honor the connection between partners and an acknowledgment that both voices matter in the relationship journey.

As we conclude this exploration of dialogue's power, consider this a call to action: Engage with your partner in open conversations. Dare to be vulnerable. Seek understanding rather than winning arguments. Whether through structured guides or spontaneous moments, the simple act of talking can transform the course of love, leading you both toward a future rich in emotional intimacy and shared dreams.

The journey of communication in relationships is ongoing and evolving. It requires effort, patience, and practice, but the rewards are immeasurable. As you prioritize dialogue in your relationship, remember that each honest conversation is a stepping stone, reinforcing the foundation of your love. Embrace the transformative potential of dialogue, and witness your connection flourish in ways you never thought possible.

Navigating Compromise

The Art of Compromise

Compromise is a cornerstone of any healthy relationship, a subtle art that blends understanding, negotiation, and genuine connection. It is not merely a tactical maneuver in a conflict but a fundamental process that allows partners to find common ground, nurture their bond, and foster a sense of harmony within their union. Yet, the path to successful compromise can be fraught with challenges—the difference between healthy compromise and unhealthy sacrifice can often seem blurred. As couples navigate the territory of differing opinions, desires, and expectations, the art of compromise becomes both a necessity and a skill. It is here that we explore how to distinguish between the two forms, understand their implications, and cultivate a habit of productive compromise that promotes mutual growth and fulfillment.

The essence of healthy compromise lies in the balance it creates. Partners who engage in healthy compromise assess each other's needs and desires while considering the relationship's overall well-being. They understand that effective compromise does not mean simply surrendering one's own wishes for the sake of placating the other. Instead, it is about arriving at a solution that honors both perspectives, ensuring that both partners feel heard and valued. For example, consider Ella and Adam, a couple facing a decision about where to spend their summer vacation. Ella longs for a serene beach experience, while Adam prefers an action-packed mountain getaway. After discussing their individual preferences, they opt for a compromise: a week at a beach destination that includes opportunities for hiking and exploring nearby trails. This decision reflects not only a balance of interests but also showcases their willingness to prioritize each other's happiness—a hallmark of healthy compromise.

On the other hand, unhealthy sacrifice manifests when one partner consistently places the needs of the other above their own to the point of resentment. Unhealthy compromise often results in one partner feeling neglected or overburdened, as their vital needs continue to go unaddressed. It can lead to significant emotional turmoil and eventually erode the relationship's foundations. David and Sarah present a cautionary tale in this regard. Sarah, who has always wanted to start a family, finds herself constantly agreeing to David's wish to postpone parenthood for his career ambitions. She suppresses her longing for motherhood, believing that supporting David's dreams is an act of love. Over time, however, Sarah's unresolved feelings begin to fracture their bond. The resentment builds until one day, an emotionally charged argument reveals the underlying tension that had been festering beneath the surface. Their story illustrates the dangers of compromising one's core desires for the sake of creating harmony.

Navigating the landscape of compromise requires self-awareness and clear communication. It begins with recognizing one's own desires and limits—an essential step in fostering honest negotiation. When partners are aware of what they want and need, they can engage in healthy discussions aimed at understanding one another. Consider Mia and Leo, who learn this early in their relationship. They both acknowledge different perspectives on financial management: Mia is cautious and prefers saving, while Leo enjoys spending on experiences. Instead of masking their differences, they agree to set aside time every month to openly discuss their finances, taking turns to express their preferences and concerns. Their willingness to embrace vulnerability creates a breeding ground for empathy, understanding, and eventually a shared financial plan that satisfies both their urges—this confirms that healthy compromise is rooted in proactive communication.

To achieve successful compromise, it is essential to approach negotiations with an open mind and a collaborative attitude. Couples should strive to cultivate a sense of teamwork rather than an adversarial stance, focusing on resolutions that leave both parties feeling fulfilled rather than shortchanged. A practical exercise that can aid this process is to list the pros and cons of each option being considered. By visualizing the benefits and drawbacks, partners gain clarity on their priorities, and it becomes easier to understand which aspects hold significance for the relationship's overall health. This method not only invites structural discussions but also reinforces the notion that every decision made should aim to strengthen their partnership.

Empathy plays a critical role in the art of compromise. Rather than simply recognizing another person's feelings, partners must actively engage with and validate those emotions. An example arises when Jordan and Taylor find themselves at odds over a significant life event: choosing to relocate for a new job opportunity. Taylor feels excited about the prospect, while Jordan worries about leaving behind a cherished community. While negotiations initially become choppy and filled with tension, they shift toward listening deeply. As Taylor expresses the excitement of a new adventure and Jordan shares the fear of starting over, they both come to realize the depth of their feelings. Ultimately, they reach a decision to visit potential neighborhoods together before fully committing—a compromise that respects both Taylor's ambition and Jordan's apprehension. Their experience underscores how mutual empathy can guide partners to decisions that nurture the relationship rather than fracture it.

However, it is important to acknowledge that each compromise carries its own emotional weight. Some decisions may be driven by genuine desires, while others may stem from external pressures or lingering insecurities. When navigating challenging compromises, partners should be vigilant to avoid the "tug-of-war" mentality where each believes they must outmaneuver the other. In seeking balance, the goal should be restoration rather than competition. Farah and Chris, another couple, demonstrate this beautifully amid their struggle to handle a blended family situation. By prioritizing open dialogues, they can assess their differing parenting styles and expectations for their children without feeling attacked or undermined. They engage in a series of family meetings, jointly establishing a set of blended family guidelines that honors both of their approaches. Their story exemplifies how fostering a collaborative mindset enables couples to build rather than dismantle their bond.

Recognizing patterns in conflict can also inform how to approach compromise. Each couple will have unique dynamics, just as no two arguments will unfold identically. For instance, some couples may realize that certain discussions lead to repetitive patterns of passivity or aggression. By observing such tendencies, partners can proactively identify how to sidestep pitfalls. Sam and Jamie recognize that when disagreements arise regarding personal time, Jamie tends to retreat, while Sam steps up in anger. Upon recognizing this cycle, they choose to recalibrate their approach, committing to express their feelings without resorting to defensiveness. Through this process of attribution, the couple learns to recognize their triggers and preemptively address conflict collaboratively. Their journey illuminates the idea that compromise is not an endpoint but a continuous process that adapts and evolves as the relationship matures.

Achieving balance through compromise is often about ensuring both partners feel appreciated in their partnership. Emotional validation creates an environment where individuals feel seen by their partner, helping to ensure that no one's contributions go unnoticed. Take the case of Olivia and Mark, a couple navigating a complex decision regarding household chores. While Olivia prefers a tidy environment, Mark is more relaxed about messes. After several heated arguments about their differing standards, they agree to a solution: a chore chart that breaks down each task. Additionally, they build a ritual around celebrating successes by acknowledging each other's efforts. This practice cultivates an appreciation for each contribution—delivering validation to both parties that enhances overall satisfaction with the arrangement. When partners voice appreciation for their efforts, it strengthens the bond and reinforces the health of the compromise.

As couples continue to explore the art of compromise, they should remember that it is not merely a one-time discussion but an ongoing commitment. Relationships starkly differ from transactional agreements;

thus, couples must be prepared to return to the drawing board, re-evaluating decisions as circumstances shift. For example, Sarah and Robert regularly revisit their work-life balance since Sarah's job became more demanding. They make it a tradition to check in every few months, discussing what is working and what requires adjustment. Their evolving approach illustrates how healthy compromise adapts over time to the changing landscape of the relationship, nurturing their connection through shared goals and growth.

Moreover, embracing the idea that both partners can bring solutions enhances the path to compromise. When conflict arises, it often helps to collaboratively brainstorm alternatives beyond the original proposals. Diversity in solution generation can spark creativity and bring surprising resolutions to light. In the case of Jenna and Greg, they find themselves at an impasse regarding their living arrangements. While Jenna wishes to purchase a home in the suburbs, Greg prefers the excitement of urban living. Instead of rigidly defending their positions, they invite suggestions from each other. They explore options such as cohabiting in an artistically vibrant neighborhood with potential for serenity and community warmth. By exploring various ideas and gathering input, they arrive at a compromise that honors both of their values.

The transformative power of compromise extends beyond immediate conflict resolution; it serves as a catalyst for personal development. As partners navigate their differences, they often discover more profound insights into themselves and each other. Compromise necessitates distinction between preferences and fixed identities, which can create space for growth. When Sara and Glen face a decision about attending a major family event, both have differing approaches to family engagement. Sara feels obligated to attend due to family tradition, while Glen expresses a desire to remain home for rest. This disagreement invites vulnerability as they openly express their underlying fears and anxieties about family dynamics. Through this process, they uncover shared values regarding family, tradition, and self-care. Ultimately, they decide to attend the event but commit to a staggered approach, allowing for a balance of family commitment and personal well-being. Their experience highlights how compromise expands individual understanding as it nurtures the relationship.

Ultimately, the art of compromise shapes the trajectory of a relationship. Healthy compromise requires intention, reflection, empathy, and communication, providing space for both partners to feel valued, heard, and understood. Over time, as couples hone their skills in compromise, they learn to navigate the complexities of their union, generating deeper connections, mutual respect, and sincere affection. Whether it is about grand life decisions or the minutiae of daily living, compromise fosters the understanding that love is not just about individual priorities but about mutual growth and partnership.

As couples continue their journeys, the commitment to the art of compromise invites them to embrace the evolving nature of their relationship, finding balance and harmony in their shared lives. In the end, the art of compromise becomes an essential skill for those seeking a thriving relationship—a gentle reminder that love flourishes not in the absence of conflict but in the grace of compromise, where understanding and connection reign supreme.

Maintaining Individuality in Partnership

In many relationships, the excitement of being in love often creates a sense of urgency to merge lives completely. Couples can inadvertently start to lose touch with their individual identities in the process of building a shared life. This loss, sometimes subtle and other times pronounced, can lead to feelings of resentment, frustration, and disconnection. However, a healthy partnership does not require sacrificing one's individuality—rather, it flourishes when both partners are able to grow and thrive as individuals while also nurturing their connection.

The importance of maintaining individuality within a partnership cannot be overstated. Individuality is not merely about personal preferences or tastes; it encompasses one's values, passions, and ambitions. When partners honor and support each other's unique identities, it cultivates an environment where both individuals can flourish. This flourishing promotes a sense of fulfillment that enriches the partnership itself.

Supporting one another's personal growth begins with open and honest communication about each person's hopes, dreams, and aspirations. Each partner should feel comfortable expressing their needs without fear of judgment. This can be accomplished through deep conversations in a safe and loving environment. For instance, engaging in periodic "state of the union" discussions can serve as a dedicated time to check in with each other about personal goals and the relationship itself. By approaching these conversations from a place of curiosity and support, couples can effectively engage with the individual narratives that shape their partnership.

Consider the narrative of Emma and Jake, a couple who initially merged their lives swiftly after falling in love. Emma was an aspiring artist while Jake was passionate about his technology career. Early in their relationship, they gravitated toward mutual interests, often engaging in activities they both enjoyed. However, before long, Jake began to prioritize his work, often encouraging Emma to give up some of her art shows to help him with his projects. Although this seemed practical at the time, Emma started to feel unfulfilled, questioning her sense of self and the reasons she had put her artistic pursuits on hold.

As resentment bubbled beneath the surface, Emma decided to be open about her feelings in one of their check-ins. She expressed her deep desire to pursue her art and sought Jake's support rather than his opposition. Surprisingly, this revelation created a breakthrough in their relationship. Jake realized that he had unintentionally stifled Emma's passion in the name of practicality. Instead of viewing her artistic aspirations as burdensome, he began to appreciate them as critical components of Emma's personality.

Once they came to this understanding, they agreed to prioritize individual pursuits alongside their relationship. Jake encouraged Emma to attend art workshops, even assisting her in promoting her art shows on social media. In turn, Emma became Jake's biggest champion, celebrating his career milestones and providing encouragement during his stressful work phases. By maintaining their individuality, both partners became happier and more fulfilled, enriching their relationship along the way.

Emphasizing one's individuality does not mean retreating into separate worlds, but rather fostering a connection that allows each individual to pursue their own interests, friendships, and ambitions. One practical strategy couples can adopt is to maintain separate hobbies or interests that do not necessarily involve their partner. Whether it's joining a book club, taking a cooking class, or engaging in fitness activities separately, these pursuits can enhance personal satisfaction and help retain a sense of self. Viewing these interests as part of a balanced relationship can provide both partners with new experiences to share and discuss, stimulating deeper conversations and connections.

Jessica and Mark illustrate this principle beautifully. Both in their thirties, they initially enjoyed doing everything together, from going to the gym to attending social events. However, over time, Mark felt increasingly constrained by the pressure to be Jessica's constant companion. On the other hand, Jessica began to feel stifled by the constant expectations of participation. After realizing their mounting dissatisfaction, they sought a compromise: they would encourage each other to take on separate activities that nurtured their individuality. Jessica decided to take a pottery class, while Mark joined a hiking club.

During the initial weeks apart, they both experienced the thrill of new accomplishments and meeting new friends. They would return home with anecdotes about their respective experiences.

Jessica often delighted in sharing her creations from pottery class, while Mark would recite the tales of his hiking trails. These "separate" experiences filled their conversations with new energy and richness, and soon they learned that not only was their individuality thriving, but their relationship also deepened as they discovered new dimensions of each other's personalities.

Another critical component of maintaining individuality in a partnership is encouraging growth and change. Just as individuals change throughout their lives, so too do relationships mature and evolve. Supporting each other in navigating these changes takes patience, understanding, and, crucially, a willingness to redefine partnership as one that celebrates growth—rather than as a static arrangement where roles and expectations are fixed.

Growth can manifest in various ways; it may stem from professional development, personal exploration, or shifts in social circles. Supporting these changes requires open dialogues about evolving identities and new aspirations. This proactive communication can lay the groundwork for ongoing discussions about how the partnership can adapt to incorporate these monumental shifts.

Take, for example, the situation of Amir and Sara. As Amir advanced in his marketing career, he began to feel the calling to speak publicly and lead workshops on personal development. Initially, this shift created friction between the couple; Sara, who had a steady job in education, felt anxious about Amir's increasing social obligations and expansion of their social circles. Instead of allowing this discomfort to fester, they chose to address it head-on during their regular relationship check-ins.

Amir shared his excitement about his new venture, explaining how important it was for him to explore this facet of his character. Sara, while concerned about potential shifts in their time together, gradually grew to appreciate Amir's passion. Together, they committed to setting aside time for their own pursuits; Amir could devote time to his speaking engagements while Sara continued to develop her educational practices at work. Through check-ins and adjustments, they created a co-support system that celebrated each person's unique journey, ultimately fostering a stronger bond between them.

Another delineation between healthy individuality and self-absorption is recognizing the difference between pursuing personal goals and disregarding the importance of the partnership. While it is essential to pursue individual passions, it is equally important not to neglect shared experiences, connection, and mutual support. Finding harmony between individuality and partnership requires intentionally creating space for shared goals and experiences alongside personal ones.

Consider how the balance between individual visions and collective aspirations can play out in the context of family planning. When couples begin to navigate significant life decisions together—such as parenting, purchasing a home, or career changes—they should prioritize understanding each other's perspectives. This can be a delicate balancing act. For instance, two partners may find themselves at odds on philosophical approaches to parenting.

This is where the merit of maintaining individuality within the context of partnership becomes apparent. Sarah, a lawyer with robust ambitions, and Daniel, a freelance artist, had differing ideas about parenting. Sarah envisioned a structured, goal-oriented upbringing, while Daniel wanted to foster creativity and freedom. Instead of planting their flags and sticking to their stances, they engaged in open discussions that laid the groundwork for understanding each other's motivations. By acknowledging one another's backgrounds, values, and desires, they patiently crafted a hybrid approach that encompassed both structure and creativity.

In reviewing their compromise, it became evident that maintaining their individuality in perspective was crucial to finding common ground in parenting. Daniel learned to appreciate the value of structure embedded in Sarah's approach, while Sarah began to see the benefits of creativity and flexibility. This process echoed the underlying pattern prevalent in many successful partnerships: a deep commitment to understanding that individuality ultimately enhances the shared journey.

To proactively foster individuality while building connection, couples can implement specific practices that nurture both aspects of their relationship. Some practical strategies include:

1. Establishing Regular Check-Ins: Scheduled discussions about personal goals, relationships needs, and changes are vital for fostering ongoing communication. These sessions should allow both individuals the space to voice their aspirations and concerns.

2. Encouraging Each Other's Interests: Take the time to

support each other's hobbies, projects, and passions—attending events, providing assistance, or simply being an encouraging listener.

3. Setting Boundaries: Recognize that it may be necessary to define boundaries around time and energy spent together versus separately. Reassess shared routines and obligations to ensure each partner can prioritize personal growth.

4. Celebrating Achievements: Acknowledge and celebrate individual successes, no matter how small. Whether it's a milestone at work or an art piece completed, celebrations can reinforce the significance of each person's identity.

5. Allocating Quality Time Together: To balance individuality with partnership, invest in dedicated quality time together—as a couple or family. Date nights, shared adventures, or simply quiet evenings at home can enhance the sense of relationship and connection in the partnership.

When approached thoughtfully, nurturing individuality can be a cornerstone of lasting love. By maintaining their unique identities, partners can avoid the pitfalls of losing themselves in the relationship—creating a union enriched by the strengths of both individuals, rather than diminished by convergence. Relationships thrive on diversity; when both partners are encouraged to realize their full potential, the partnership becomes a mirror reflecting the best versions of each individual.

As we examine the intricate interplay between

individuality and partnership, it is clear that authentic connections do not stifle personal growth, but rather encourage it. Individuals can embark on their journeys and evolve as their authentic selves—all while maintaining a loving, supportive relationship that champions their shared commitment to each other. The rewards of this balanced approach reveal themselves in the joy of reconnecting with oneself and fostering a deeper, more satisfying connection with one's partner. In doing so, both people in the relationship can flourish, leading to a more meaningful and enriching partnership that stands the test of time.

Creating Win-Win Solutions

In relationships, compromise is often viewed as a necessary evil, a give-and-take dynamic that requires individuals to relinquish something they want for the sake of harmony. However, compromise does not have to be a bitter pill to swallow. Through the pursuit of win-win solutions, couples can transform compromises into collaborative victories that benefit both partners, promoting deeper understanding, respect, and connection. This approach allows for imaginative negotiation that preserves individuality while fostering partnership.

In this subchapter, we will explore the fundamentals of creating win-win solutions in relationships and provide practical frameworks that can help guide you and your partner toward outcomes that are mutually beneficial. As we navigate the landscape of compromise, we will focus on several core principles that can cultivate a wealth of possibilities. Engaging questions will be posed to stimulate introspection and self-awareness, allowing for personal growth and a healthier, more fulfilling partnership.

To begin, it is essential to understand what win-win solutions entail. At its core, creating a win-win outcome means finding a resolution to a disagreement that meets the needs and desires of both individuals involved. Instead of viewing conflict through a lens of scarcity—believing that one partner's gain necessitates the other's loss—win-win solutions operate within a framework of abundance. They require partners to appreciate each other's perspectives, explore the depths of their respective needs, and creatively brainstorm options that reconcile differences.

One foundational principle of creating win-win solutions is open communication. Effective dialogue lays the groundwork for any collaborative effort. Expressing feelings and needs candidly can dismantle the barriers that often accompany disagreements. To foster effective communication, both partners must practice active listening, which involves not merely hearing the words spoken, but engaging with the underlying emotions and intentions.

For example, consider a couple, Sarah and Tom, who find themselves at an impasse concerning weekend plans. Tom wants to spend Saturday with his friends while Sarah wishes to spend quality time together. If Tom hears Sarah's request as a demand rather than a meaningful expression of desire, he might respond defensively, leading to a standoff. Instead, if he practices active listening, he can frame his response around empathy and curiosity. By asking open-ended questions, such as, "What do you hope to get from that time together?" he uncovers deeper feelings behind Sarah's request, and they can explore solutions that honor both of their desires.

Open communication creates safe spaces where partners feel comfortable sharing their truths. This type of environment encourages vulnerability, allowing for authentic expression without fear of judgment or retaliation. Vulnerability is a crucial aspect of successful negotiation in which each partner communicates their feelings, needs, and priorities clearly while remaining open to understanding the other's perspective.

Once open communication is established, partners can begin exploring options for compromise. A critical step in this process is brainstorming alternatives. It's helpful to approach this phase with a mindset that is free from preconceived notions about what a "resolution" looks like. Instead of focusing on one ideal outcome, couples can consider a range of possibilities, expanding the solution space.

Using the earlier example of Sarah and Tom, once they communicate their needs, they may brainstorm various alternatives together. They could agree to spend Saturday afternoon with Tom's friends and have a romantic dinner afterward, or perhaps they decide to plan an alternate weekend that prioritizes their time together. By keeping an open heart and mind, they transform a potential conflict into an opportunity for creativity and collaboration.

One of the frameworks that can facilitate the creation of win-win solutions is the "Interest-Based Relational Approach" (IBRA). This approach posits that individuals should prioritize interests rather than positions. When partners take positions, they become entrenched in their views and unwilling to consider other perspectives. Instead, by focusing on interests—the underlying reasons for those positions—couples can identify common ground.

For instance, in a discussion around financial budgeting, one partner may feel justified in insisting on savings while the other prioritizes spending on enjoyable experiences. Here, the positions diverge: one is focused on saving for the future (position), while the other desires present enjoyment. However, if both partners articulate their interests—security versus enjoyment—they can explore various solutions, such as creating a budget that allocates funds for savings while also designating a portion for leisure activities. This collaborative approach ensures that both partners' interests are heard and addressed, enabling them to find harmony in their differing perspectives.

Another effective framework is the "Win-Win Negotiation Model," which consists of several stages that guide partners through the process of achieving shared solutions. The steps include:

1. Preparation: Before discussions, each partner should assess their needs and desires independently. Questions to consider include: What do I need? What are my priorities? What could I be flexible about?

2. Discussion: In this stage, partners engage in active listening and open communication, sharing their individual needs while remaining receptive to hearing their partner's thoughts.

3. Exploration: Together, partners brainstorm potential solutions, drawing on creativity and open-

mindedness. This is where both partners can feel free to share ideas that might initially seem unrealistic, as the point is to expand the exploration.

4. Evaluation: Partners assess the feasibility of the brainstormed solutions—keeping in mind each other's interests—and narrow down potential win-win solutions that meet their needs.

5. Implementation: Once a solution is agreed upon, partners collaboratively establish how they will put it into action. Consideration should be given to both partners' roles in executing the agreement.

6. Review: After implementation, it's vital to revisit the solution to ensure both partners are satisfied with the outcome and to discuss any necessary modifications.

The journey of compromise is one of mutual growth, and employing these frameworks gives partners practical tools to navigate challenges constructively.

Engaging questions serve as a vital component of self-reflection during the compromise process. By encouraging introspection, these questions empower individuals to examine their attitudes toward compromise and their role within their partnership. Here are some prompts you might consider:

- What do I generally prioritize when faced with a disagreement? Is it my needs, my partner's needs, or the relationship as a whole?
- Have I approached recent disagreements with a

collaborative mindset? If not, what barriers prevented me from doing so?
- How do I define a successful compromise in my relationship, and does this align with my partner's understanding of success in compromise?
- Have I communicated my feelings clearly in past negotiations, or have I relied on assumptions or silent resentments?
- What were the outcomes of previous compromises? How did I feel about those outcomes, and what can I learn from them moving forward?

The answers to these questions can provide insight into personal patterns that may hinder the pursuit of win-win solutions. By recognizing and addressing these internal dynamics, individuals can become more empowered partners who contribute positively to their relationship landscape.

Moreover, embracing win-win solutions nurtures a culture of respect and understanding between partners. It honors the individuality of each partner while simultaneously reinforcing the commitment to shared goals. As couples move through disagreements with a spirit of collaboration, they deepen their connection and solidify their partnership.

Creating a space for win-win solutions does require effort from both partners. Sometimes, this means stepping outside of one's comfort zone, relinquishing the "right" to be heard first, or challenging oneself to be more open-minded. And just as critical, it often necessitates a sincere willingness to let go of stubbornness and embrace flexibility. When both partners commit to this approach, the potential for growth within the relationship is monumental.

As we conclude this exploration into creating win-win compromises, let us embrace the empowerment that comes from navigating differences with intention and collaboration. Relationships naturally ebb and flow through challenges and disagreements, yet the transformative power of seeking win-win solutions can illuminate pathways previously obscured by conflict. By prioritizing communication, curiosity, and creativity, couples can cultivate an ecosystem of understanding, respect, and love—essential ingredients for lasting partnerships.

The journey ahead is one of continual learning, not just about each other, but about oneself. As you engage in this ongoing process, may your commitment to seek healthy compromises lead you toward the profound connections you desire. In doing so, expect not only personal growth but also a vibrant partnership that evolves and thrives, rooted in mutual understanding and respect. The power of negotiation—of unifying your voices into a harmonious song of compromise—awaits you.

The Future of Marriage

Evolving Trends in Relationships

As society continues to evolve, so too does the fabric of relationships and marriage. This subchapter examines significant trends that are reshaping the institution of marriage, bringing to light new norms and evolving values. From increased acceptance of cohabitation before marriage to the delay of marriage in favor of personal development and career growth, these shifts reflect broader societal changes. Additionally, the evolution of gender roles plays a critical role in how partnerships are formed and sustained today.

One of the most notable trends in recent years is the rise of cohabitation. Once stigmatized and limited to certain demographics, living together before marriage has become an accepted practice for many couples. According to a recent study by the Pew Research Center, approximately 59% of adults in the United States believe that cohabitation is a viable alternative to marriage. This marks a significant departure from traditional views that only sanctioned marriage as a legitimate bond. Cohabitation offers couples a unique opportunity to assess compatibility in a shared living environment while reducing financial risks associated with marriage.

This trend toward cohabitation is often framed within the larger context of evolving attitudes toward commitment. Whereas previous generations might have seen marriage as the first and foremost step in a relationship, modern couples tend to view it as part of an ongoing negotiation. Many young adults prioritize establishing stability in their relationships before formalizing their commitment through marriage. 'The Researcher' emphasizes that this shift is not merely about living arrangements; it represents a broader cultural change that reflects shifts in belief about commitment, partnership, and what it means to be a couple in the 21st century.

However, the trend toward cohabitation isn't without its challenges. Many couples find themselves grappling with issues related to financial dependency, responsibility sharing, and parental expectations. A relevant narrative comes from Simone and Jordan, a couple who lived together for several years before deciding to marry. They enjoyed the benefits of sharing expenses and co-managing household responsibilities, but they often found themselves in conflict over issues such as chores and financial spending. "We loved each other, but we realized that living together was a whole different ball game compared to just dating. The compromises we had to make expanded into previously uncharted territories," Simone shares. Their journey illustrates both the value of cohabitation for compatibility testing as well as the complexities that arise when intimate partners share responsibilities.

Delayed marriage is another significant trend that has reshaped the landscape of relationships. In decades past, marriage typically took place in the early twenties, but contemporary cultural developments have led many individuals to delay this milestone in favor of personal fulfillment, education, and career advancement. The average age of first marriage in the United States has risen from about 23 for women and 26 for men in 1970 to approximately 30 for women and 32 for men today. This substantial shift in age reflects a wider acceptance of the idea that personal development—whether in terms of education, career, or personal identity—is crucial before taking the step into matrimony.

This trend can be attributed to multiple factors including economic pressures, the pursuit of higher education, and the desire for self-exploration. 'The Researcher' points out that as young adults delay marriage, they are also more likely to seek out long-term partnerships without the traditional title of "husband" or "wife." This quest for personal development allows individuals to establish a sense of self that will ultimately benefit future partnerships. The narrative of Maya and Tom exemplifies this journey. Both chose to complete their graduate studies and establish their careers before making any commitments. "We wanted to understand who we were first, separate from each other," Maya reflects. "It created a strong foundation in our relationship, and when we finally got engaged, it felt right because we knew it was about both of us, not just societal expectations."

The evolution of gender roles is also transforming relationships, as contemporary partnerships strive for a more egalitarian structure. Traditional notions of marriage often relied on rigid gender roles, placing expectations on men as providers and women as caretakers. In today's world, many couples adopt more fluid roles, leading to collaborative decision-making and shared responsibilities. This shift allows for greater autonomy and fulfillment, as both partners can pursue their aspirations while maintaining a supportive home environment.

Studies indicate that couples who embrace

egalitarian relationships report a higher level of satisfaction and stability in their marriages. By participating in household duties and finances equally, partners cultivate a sense of team spirit, where shared responsibilities reflect a partnership rather than a hierarchical structure. 'The Researcher' notes that as gender expectations continue to change, we will likely see a rise in diverse family structures and partnership agreements that defy traditional norms, thus enriching the fabric of familial relationships. The experiences of Nicole and Eli encapsulate this trend, as both partners share responsibilities in their domestic life and child-rearing. "We both work full-time, and we didn't want one of us to feel overwhelmed with household tasks while the other focused solely on work," Nicole notes. Their story demonstrates how an equal division of labor not only builds resilience in a relationship but also creates an emotional bond strengthened by collaboration.

While these emerging trends provide a promising outlook for the future of marriage, they are not without complications. As partners grapple with ever-changing societal norms and the realities of modern life, many couples face important questions about compatibility, values, and commitment. The narratives shared illustrate the need for open communication and evidence of emotional maturity to navigate these changes successfully. Couples who embrace a growth mindset, learning and adapting together, are often the ones who thrive amidst these shifts.

The impact of technology on relationships also calls for exploration within the landscape of evolving trends. In today's digital age, the ways in which people meet, court, and communicate have been fundamentally altered. Online dating apps have democratized the dating landscape, allowing individuals from diverse backgrounds to connect in ways that were previously unimaginable. While this can facilitate a broader range of options for prospective partners, it also raises challenges related to superficiality and commitment. 'The Researcher' suggests that technology has the power to enhance relationships when used mindfully, promoting deeper emotional connections rather than superficial interactions.

Consider the story of Sarah and Raj, who met through a dating app and quickly fell in love. Their relationship began with a whirlwind of late-night conversations, virtual dates, and shared playlists. Despite their initial excitement, navigating their relationship was challenging. "We found ourselves caught up in a cycle of texting but struggled to communicate meaningful emotions," Sarah admits. "It wasn't until we made a conscious effort to invest time in in-person interactions that our bond deepened." Their experience reinforces the idea that although technology can ease the path to connections, it is the quality and depth of interaction that ultimately sustains relationships.

The increasing acceptance of same-sex marriage and partnerships has also had a profound impact on the landscape of relationships. As legal barriers have been dismantled and societal perceptions continue to shift, many LGBTQ+ couples have achieved the dignity and recognition they deserve. This landmark change has not only provided same-sex couples with the same rights to marry but has also fostered a culture of acceptance and understanding towards diverse relationships. The journey of Ada and Mia reflects this paradigm shift. "When we married, it felt like a culmination of so much struggle and advocacy," Ada recalls. Their relationship has evolved within the context of societal change, affirming the idea that love takes many forms and should be celebrated.

As we examine these evolving trends, it is crucial to maintain a perspective grounded in awareness and authenticity. The complexities of modern relationships call for emotional maturity, communication, trust, and respect for individuality. Couples can reap the rewards of evolving societal values by fostering an environment of growth and mutual support, leading to lasting connections.

In conclusion, the landscape of marriage and relationships is undergoing significant transformation, informed by societal changes, technological advancements, and evolving gender roles.

The trend towards cohabitation, delayed marriage, and egalitarian partnerships reflects broader cultural shifts that embrace individual growth and redefine love and commitment. Narratives from couples navigating these changes illustrate the importance of communication and adaptation in fostering enduring relationships. As society continues to evolve, so too must our understanding of love, partnership, and the future of marriage itself. The power lies not only in recognizing these trends but also in the intentional choices couples make to cultivate authentic connections that resonate with their unique values and aspirations.

Redefining Commitment

In the contemporary landscape of love and relationships, the concept of commitment is undergoing a profound transformation. While traditional definitions of marriage often centered on the notion of lifelong monogamy and the cultural scripts that accompanied it, the modern era is witnessing a diversification of relationships that challenge these conventions. What does it mean to be committed in an age where love can take myriad forms? This subchapter delves into evolving definitions of commitment, exploring alternative relationship structures and the increasing acceptance of non-traditional unions.

Historically, marriage has often been regarded as the ultimate expression of commitment—a societal expectation steeped in religious, familial, and cultural significance. Yet, what happens when individuals begin to recognize that love is not confined to one framework? As societal norms shift, so too do the understandings of what it means to commit to another person. The rise of cohabitation, same-sex unions, polyamorous relationships, and non-monogamous arrangements illustrates the desire for more personalized, meaningful connections that transcend traditional boundaries.

A growing body of research indicates that younger generations view relationships through a more flexible lens. For many, engaging in relationships is less about subscribing to societal expectations and more about creating spaces where love is genuine, fulfilling, and tailored to individual needs. Millennials and Generation Z are leading this change, with their openness to diverse relationship structures signaling a move away from the rigid confines of tradition.

To better understand these evolving definitions of commitment, we turn our attention to individuals navigating alternative relationship structures. Through interviews, we uncover the stories of people who are redefining their understanding of love and commitment based on their unique experiences and desires.

Isabella and Sarah have been together for five years and have chosen to navigate their commitment outside the traditional bounds of marriage. As a same-sex couple living in an urban environment, they emphasize authenticity in their relationship. "For us, commitment isn't tied to a ring or a certificate," Isabella explains. "It's about the emotional bond we share and how we cultivate our life together." Isabella and Sarah have crafted a relationship that prioritizes growth and flexibility. They've openly discussed the possibility of exploring connections with other partners while maintaining their core commitment to each other.

This brings us to the concept of polyamory, which challenges conventional ideas of exclusivity and loyalty. James and Marcus, a couple in their early thirties, have embraced a polyamorous arrangement that allows them to connect romantically with others while still fostering a deep partnership with each other. "Commitment in our relationship isn't about inhibiting each other's personal growth," says James. "It's about supporting each other in our pursuits of love and connection with others." Their relationship centers on communication, trust, and mutual respect, highlighting that commitment can indeed coexist with love for multiple partners.

As these personal stories unfold, it's clear that commitment has come to be understood as fluid, dynamic, and layered. For many, the complexity of non-traditional unions fosters a deeper understanding of love itself. Commitment can manifest in countless forms—each imbued with its own unique depth and meaning.

One significant development in the landscape of commitment is the rise in cohabitation among couples who choose to share their lives without formalizing their relationship through marriage. Sofia and Ethan, both in their late twenties, have been living together for two years. They cite their commitment to each other as a shared partnership built on trust, collaboration, and communication. "We don't see the need to get married just to prove our love," Ethan explains. "We're committed to building a life together, and that feels enough for us."

Cohabitation often provides couples with a practical avenue for testing compatibility, allowing them to experience the dynamics of shared life without formal obligations tied to marriage. This shift toward living together without the marriage label signifies a reevaluation of tradition—a freedom to establish relationships based on what individuals genuinely desire, rather than conforming to societal expectations.

Another poignant example of evolving commitment can be observed in the realm of long-distance relationships. Emma and Ray, separated by thousands of miles, have cultivated a deep commitment despite geographical distance. "We understand that commitment doesn't necessarily require physical proximity," Emma notes. "Our love is built on trust and shared experiences, even if they're virtual for now." Their journey challenges the conventional idea that marriage must be co-located. They've developed a personalized approach to their relationship—setting goals, planning visits, and finding creative ways to maintain intimacy across the miles. This illustrates that commitment can transcend physical boundaries, adjusting to circumstances while remaining deeply rooted in emotional connection.

As we explore the shifting definitions of commitment, it is clear that the new terrain requires a commitment to open-mindedness and understanding. The narratives of Isabella and Sarah, James and Marcus, Sofia and Ethan, and Emma and Ray serve as illustrative examples of how diverse relationships manifest and thrive despite societal perceptions. The cross-pollination of ideas—from unwavering commitment to embracing flexibility—invites readers to reflect on their own beliefs about commitment.

This reflection can lead to critical questioning: What does commitment look like for us? Is it about adhering to traditional markers, or is it about creating a partnership that aligns with our authentic selves? Most importantly, is it built upon shared values and emotional connections?

Embracing open dialogue about commitment allows individuals to explore their unique relational needs and desires. The journey toward understanding one's own beliefs about commitment can be empowering, fostering growth and deeper connections. Couples are encouraged to communicate openly about their definitions of love and commitment, leading to relationships that feel authentic and supportive.

While the modern landscape of commitment may appear fragmented and expansive, it's essential to remember that each individual's journey is valid, worthy, and deserving of respect. The evolving definitions aim to liberate love from existing constraints, offering a refreshing perspective: love is not bound by tradition but can be shaped through the desires and choices of those involved.

Importantly, the increasing acceptance of non-traditional unions fosters a culture in which inclusivity and diversity flourish. As society progresses, many individuals have begun to question the traditional marriage framework in favor of alternative relationship structures—challenging long-held dogmas and prejudices.

Navigating the complexities of such varied commitments requires conscious effort, emotional intelligence, and a willingness to empathize with others' experiences. Discussions around commitment become richer when diverse voices are heard—when the stories of different partnerships come to the forefront, allowing for a deeper exploration of how commitment can manifest.

Understanding that commitment can flourish in many forms opens the door for a broader conversation about love, respect, and agency in relationships. The recognition that individuals deserve to define their own path transforms the notion of commitment from a rigid institution into a landscape filled with possibility.

As we reflect on the future of love and commitment in this evolving social context, there remains hope that each individual can find a path that resonates with them, free from the constraints imposed by history. The new paradigm encourages individuals to cultivate their relationships intentionally, focusing on what truly matters—authentic emotional connections, mutual respect, and the freedom to create commitments that work for them.

In summary, the transformative potential of redefining commitment emerges from a willingness to adapt—to embrace diversity, challenge norms, and open one's heart to new experiences. The radical rearticulation of what commitment means to each individual serves as a beacon of hope for a future where love, in all its forms, can be nurtured and celebrated.

The Future of Love

As we stand on the cusp of a new era in romantic relationships, the landscape of love and connection is evolving at an unprecedented speed. With the rise of technology and the shifting paradigms of societal values, the ways we find, engage, and nurture romantic relationships are undergoing a revolution. This subchapter aims to speculate on the future of love, examining the profound impact that advancements in technology and changes in our social fabric may have on how we relate to one another.

Dating apps have emerged as the predominant means of meeting potential partners in modern society. In just a few short years, they have transformed from niche platforms to mainstream tools, with millions engaged in digital matchmaking. Apps like Tinder, OkCupid, and Bumble, among others, have changed the playing field, shifting the dynamics of dating. These platforms have democratized the dating experience, allowing individuals to connect with potential partners beyond their immediate social circles and geographical limitations. In this way, they have broadened the horizons of love, allowing people to explore relationships with individuals they might never have encountered otherwise.

However, while dating apps facilitate connections, they also introduce a myriad of complexities. The swipe culture that defines many of these platforms has contributed to a commodification of romantic interactions, often reducing individuals to mere profiles and photographs. This can lead to a superficial understanding of potential partners, where the depth of a person's character may be overshadowed by their avatar or biographical blurbs. As the ease of connecting with many partners increases, so does the risk of fleeting interactions that lack the emotional intimacy necessary for meaningful relationships.

Virtual relationships are another aspect of love's future that deserves attention. With advancements in technology, including virtual reality (VR) and artificial intelligence (AI), new forms of romantic connection are emerging. Imagine a world where individuals can engage in shared virtual experiences, exploring immersive environments together without physical proximity. While this may foster a sense of closeness for some, it also raises questions about the authenticity of such interactions. Can genuine love and emotional attachment be formed in purely virtual spaces, or are they inherently limited by the lack of real-world presence?

The reality is that many people are already cultivating significant relationships online. Whether through social media platforms, video calls, or immersive gaming experiences, connections are forming in digital spaces. However, these relationships can be precarious. The anonymity of the internet can prompt misrepresentation, where individuals may present curated versions of themselves, leading to misunderstandings and betrayal when these relationships move into the physical realm.

Changing communication styles also play a critical role in the future of love. As texting and instant messaging have overtaken voice calls and face-to-face conversations, the way couples communicate has evolved significantly. This shift has both positive and negative implications. On one hand, technology allows for instantaneous communication, making it easier to stay connected—even when miles apart. On the other hand, the nuances of interpersonal communication can sometimes be lost in translation. Text messages lack the tone and body language that enrich face-to-face conversations, which can result in misunderstandings and conflicts that may have been mitigated in person.

As we navigate this new terrain of love and relationships, it becomes imperative to prioritize authenticity and emotional intimacy. In a world where connections can be hastily formed and easily dismantled, the foundation of relationships must be built on genuine understanding, trust, and communication. Couples need to strive for meaningful conversations and shared experiences that transcend the digital screens that often mediate their interactions. It is through these principles that lasting love can flourish, regardless of the platforms through which connections are made.

As readers envision their future in love, they are encouraged to reflect on certain engaging questions: How do you envision your future relationships adapting to these technological advancements? Will you prioritize virtual connections, or do you gravitate toward nurturing in-person interactions? In a world where superficiality often reigns, how can you ensure that the depth of emotional connection remains central to your understanding of love?

Moreover, self-exploration becomes crucial in this brave new world of romance. Readers are urged to assess their relationship with technology: Does it enhance or hinder their ability to connect with potential partners? Reflection on these questions can empower individuals to take charge of their romantic journeys, harnessing the benefits of modern innovations while being mindful of the potential pitfalls.

The future of love is undeniably vibrant, with endless possibilities for connection and intimacy. The convergence of technology and shifting societal values presents both challenges and opportunities for individuals seeking romantic relationships. By remaining grounded in the principles of authenticity and emotional intimacy, readers can navigate this evolving landscape with intention and awareness.

As we move forward, it is vital to embrace the potential offered by new forms of connection while cultivating the deep, enriching love that comes from vulnerability and authenticity. By doing so, individuals can not only foster meaningful connections with others but also cultivate a future of love that is fulfilling, rewarding, and enduring. As technology continues to shape the way we relate to one another, let us remember that true love transcends devices and apps; it is a timeless pursuit rooted in connection, understanding, and the human experience.

The dialogue about the future of love does not end here. Each of us plays a role in influencing how relationships evolve in the years to come. Together, we can shape a future where love flourishes, adapting to the complexities of our modern world while remaining steadfast in our quest for authentic connections. As we embark on this journey, let us not merely survive the shifting tides of love but thrive amidst them, crafting narratives that celebrate the multifaceted beauty of human connection.

In envisioning the road ahead, one can imagine a world where love is not confined by traditional definitions or limited by physical spaces. The possibilities are exciting, even as we recognize the need for awareness and adaptability in our approach to relationships. Embracing technology doesn't mean sacrificing emotional depth; instead, it can serve as a tool for enriching our connections if wielded with mindfulness.

As the narrative of love continues to evolve, let us remain vigilant in maintaining a balance between innovation and intimacy. The future beckons with promise and potential, inviting us to explore, engage, and to love fully. The pursuit of joy, depth, and authenticity in our relationships should remain our guiding star, illuminating the path as we collectively navigate this evolving landscape of love. It is through our shared journeys that we can uncover new ways to express affection, establish partnerships, and ultimately, create a future of love that inspires hope and connection for generations to come.

As we conclude this exploration into the future of love, consider the legacy you wish to leave regarding your romantic connections. What stories will you share and what lessons will you impart? As technology and society continue to change at a rapid pace, let your experiences be a reflection of love's enduring nature—one that adapts, transforms, and ultimately unites us all in an intricate tapestry of human emotion and connection. Embrace the journey, for in it lies the true essence of love in all its glorious forms.

Empowerment Through Knowledge

Taking Charge of Your Relationship Journey

In the often chaotic arena of modern relationships, it's more important than ever for individuals to take charge of their own relationship journey. This subchapter, informed by the overarching themes of empowerment and self-awareness from our exploration of marriage and partnerships, serves as both a guide and a call to action. The aim is not merely to document the complexities of love but to inspire heartfelt and informed choices that allow individuals to foster authentic connections with their partners.

To embark on this journey is to acknowledge that we have agency in our relationships. The complexities of love are not just external but internal as well. Our beliefs, values, and past experiences all contribute to how we perceive love and partnership. Thus, becoming aware of these internal narratives is vital. By doing so, we forge a path toward healthier, more fulfilling relationships, grounded in understanding ourselves and what we truly seek in love.

Self-awareness is the first step. Reflect on your own relationship history. What have you learned from your past partnerships? What patterns do you notice? Many people find themselves repeating the same mistakes, falling into familiar cycles of heartache and disappointment. By recognizing these patterns, you can begin to break free from them. For example, if you find you frequently attract partners who are emotionally unavailable, ask yourself why that might be. What needs within you lead to this recurring choice? Such inquiries can be uncomfortable, but they are essential for growth.

Take the time to create a personal relationship inventory. List your strengths, weaknesses, values, and non-negotiables. This inventory isn't just a checklist; it's a profound reflection of your identity and what you desire in a partnership. Are you someone who thrives on deep emotional conversations or one who values shared activities and adventures? Perhaps you prioritize honesty above all else or yearn for deep emotional intimacy. By pinpointing these traits, you gain clarity about what you seek in a partner, leading to better compatibility.

Moreover, embracing informed decision-making is crucial in the context of romantic relationships. Too often, the decisions we make about our relationships stem from external influences—society, culture, family expectations, and even media portrayals of love. These external pressures can dilute our personal desires and shape our understanding of love and commitment in ways that are not aligned with our true selves. To counter this, it is vital to engage in active decision-making by querying every relationship choice you make. Are you with a partner because you genuinely enjoy their company, or is it due to societal pressure to settle down? Are you investing time in your relationship because of love and mutual respect, or are you simply complying with a perceived timeline?

As The Advocate would assert, each moment you invest in your relationships must align with your core beliefs. This notion requires intentionality—a conscious effort to cultivate relationships that enhance your life rather than diminish it.

Empowerment also finds its roots in understanding our desires for love and connection. For many, the desire for companionship leads them down a path where they may overlook their internal compass. To take charge means asking the tough questions. What does love mean to you? What emotions do you hope to evoke and experience in a romantic partnership? What commitments are you willing to make, and what are you unwilling to sacrifice for that partnership?

Let's explore this idea further through relatable anecdotes. Consider Sarah and David, a couple who seemed to have a picture-perfect relationship. They both had successful careers, appeared deeply in love, and were the envy of many friends. However, Sarah felt a growing sense of dissatisfaction. Deep down, she struggled with feelings of un-fulfillment and emotional disconnect.

After considerable reflection, Sarah realized that while she enjoyed David's company, she often set aside her own needs to accommodate his. The weight of societal expectations loomed large—friends and family applauded their union as a "success." Yet, what Sarah needed was to assert her desire for a deeper emotional connection. Eventually, after nurturing her self-awareness, she courageously voiced her feelings to David, transforming their relationship for the better.

Sarah's story highlights the importance of stepping back and reassessing one's relationship dynamic. By nurturing her self-awareness and embracing the notion of taking charge of her narrative, Sarah was able to foster a healthy dialogue and ultimately guide her relationship to greater intimacy—a powerful testament to the importance of empowering oneself in love.

As you navigate your own relationship journey, consider the role of values and beliefs in shaping your experiences. Are your values clearly defined? Are they shared with your partner? Deep-rooted compatibility in values forms the bedrock of any successful relationship. When two individuals share complementary values—such as how they prioritize family, career aspirations, or even how they view personal growth—they are more likely to sustain their connection over time.

After all, relationships thrive on mutual understanding and respect for one another's aspirations. To illustrate, take the case of Jenny and Mark. They both valued career success but had differing views on how to achieve a work-life balance. In time, Jenny realized that she felt unsupported in pursuing her ambitions as Mark prioritized his own goals. This realization prompted further reflection, allowing Jenny to articulate her needs while also fostering a deeper understanding of Mark's perspective.

Their experience underscores the importance of alignment in values and mutual respect. By openly discussing their priorities, Jenny and Mark forged a partnership that allowed both individuals to thrive. Taking charge of their relationship was a collaborative act that involved humility, understanding, and the willingness to adapt to one another's needs.

The journey also requires cultivating resilience. No relationship is without challenges or unresolved tensions. Emotional endurance is a quality best developed through understanding, communication, and the willingness to navigate disagreements constructively. Thus, when faced with difficulties, having established norms and responses can bolster your strength.

Think of moments of conflict. How do you respond? Do you withdraw, lash out, or engage? Healthy conflict resolution requires emotional maturity, active listening, and a genuine commitment to understanding your partner's perspective. Everyone has an emotional trigger or two—identifying these within yourself and your partner can facilitate healthier exchanges. This is the beauty of taking charge: a continuous endeavor that sharpens your conflict resolution skills.

It's also essential to realize that taking charge of your journey doesn't mean you navigate it alone. Reach out for support. Engage with friends who understand your relationship struggles, therapists who can offer professional insights, or community groups that foster emotional connections and discussions around romantic life. In many respects, shared experiences cultivate understanding and reassurance that we are not alone in our struggles.

Consider the stories of those around you. Listening to others can serve not only as a source of support but also as a means for enrichment in your own understanding of relationships. Foster deep conversations, where you go beyond surface-level topics; dig into what love means to you and the emotional layers that dictate your relational behaviors. In doing so, you'll uncover hidden insights and perhaps resonate with others' experiences that mirror your own.

In your journey toward empowerment, create a vision for love that aligns with your aspirations. Envision what your ideal partnership looks like. What makes you feel fulfilled? What daily experiences would you associate with love? Sketching a vision of your ideal relationship enables you to consciously seek out those qualities in a partner and develop the framework for nurturing them within your union.

Your vision can become a guiding star—a constant reminder of why you pursue authentic love. This vision should be both aspirational yet realistic, consisting of elements that inspire you while remaining attainable.

Reflective journaling is a powerful tool that can aid this visioning process. Allocate time to articulate your relationship goals, reflections on your day, and any insights you gather. Journaling creates a tangible output of your thoughts and desires, allowing you to revisit and adjust your vision as necessary. This practice cultivates a deeper understanding of your emotional landscape while reinforcing the notion that your journey is an empowered one.

The act of taking charge is inherently a proactive approach to personal growth. It means leaning into the discomfort of uncertainty and confronting the complexities of relationships head-on. It means being willing to learn from failures and grow from challenges rather than succumb to a victim mentality.

In concluding this subchapter, remember that your journey toward authentic love is marked by intentional choices, self-reflection, and he courage to explore uncharted territories. Embrace your agency and recognize that the course of your relationships lies within your power.

Cultivating mindfulness about your relationship journey can lead to profound transformations. The next steps include inviting transparency into your interactions and allowing your partner to join you in this journey of self-discovery. Together, you can create a partnership that thrives on mutual growth, respect, and authentic love.

As you take these lessons to heart, be inspired by Sarah, Jenny, Mark, and others who have navigated the complexities of modern relationships. Know that you are not alone, and your power to influence your journey is ever-present. Whether by reinforcing your self-awareness, embracing informed decisions, or fostering resilience, you possess the ability to enrich and empower both your life and your relationships. Start today—take charge of your relationship journey, and embark on this transformative expedition toward genuine love and fulfillment.

Creating Your Relationship Blueprint

Creating your own relationship blueprint is an essential step toward fostering the kind of love and connection you desire. This blueprint acts as a roadmap, offering clear insights into your values, goals, and aspirations for a fulfilling partnership. Just as an architect drafts a blueprint to visualize and plan a structure, you can create a detailed framework that guides your approach to relationships. By intentionally outlining what you want, you empower yourself to make informed choices, and to engage in relationships that resonate with your true self.

To embark on this journey of self-discovery, take a moment to set aside distractions and create a comforting space where you can reflect. Grab a journal or a piece of paper and prepare to answer some guided questions that will illuminate your path. These reflection prompts will help you delve into the core of your motivations as you seek to understand your relationship desires better.

Begin by contemplating your core values. Values are the guiding principles that shape your beliefs and behaviors. Ask yourself: What qualities are most important to me in a partner? What traits do I prioritize in relationships? Consider whether honesty, trust, loyalty, empathy, or adventure resonates most with you. Jot down your top five values, as they will become foundational elements in your blueprint.

Next, assess your relationship goals. What are you hoping to achieve in your love life? Are you seeking a lifelong partner, or are you currently focused on personal growth and exploration? Reflect on your long-term aspirations for a relationship. It's critical to differentiate between your desires for the present and what you envision for the future. Write down your top three relationship goals, highlighting both immediate and future aspirations, as they will help you set your intentions.

Once you have identified your core values and goals, consider the emotional needs that you yearn to fulfill in a partnership. Emotional needs can encompass various aspects, such as feeling valued, secure, fulfilled, and understood. Think about the moments in which you felt the most emotionally connected with someone. What contributed to that feeling? Conversely, recall experiences where you felt disconnected or unfulfilled. Acknowledge these feelings and describe them in detail. By understanding your emotional needs, you bring clarity to how you can seek out the support and love that will nourish your heart.

Now that you have defined your core values, goals, and emotional needs, take a moment to explore what kind of partner you envision. What attributes would this person have? Consider their interests, values, and lifestyle choices. Reflect on the experiences that have shaped your views on compatibility. Your ideal partner should complement you—someone who aligns with your values and goals while fueling your emotional needs. Write a description of this partner, capturing the essence of who you want by your side.

Next, consider the environment in which you want to cultivate your relationship. Think about the type of partnership you aspire to build, the lifestyle you envision, and where you see this connection flourishing. Are you seeking a vibrant social life where you regularly engage with others, or do you prefer quieter, more intimate moments? Imagining the backdrop of your relationship can help ground your vision, painting a clearer picture of what it looks like in practice.

As you gather these insights, take a moment to explore any limiting beliefs or fears that may hinder your ability to cultivate your ideal relationship. Acknowledging these obstacles can help you identify areas where personal growth is needed. Reflect on past experiences that may have contributed to these beliefs. Are they based on truth, or are they remnants of fear that have held you back? Write down your reflections on these limiting beliefs and formulate a plan to overcome them.

By creating this comprehensive relationship blueprint, you lay a solid foundation for your relationship journey. When faced with decisions, challenges, or new opportunities, you can refer back to your blueprint for guidance. It becomes a source of empowerment, reminding you of your core values and aspirations as you navigate the complex landscape of love and connection.

To illustrate the transformative power of intentionality in relationships, consider the story of Sarah, a 32-year-old teacher who found herself stuck in a cycle of dating people who didn't align with her values. After going through a difficult breakup, she decided to take a step back and create her relationship blueprint. Through guided reflections, Sarah discovered that her top values were trust, growth, and adventure. She realized that her previous partners often lacked these qualities, leading to discontentment.

Focusing on her relationship goals, Sarah articulated that she wanted a committed partner who was open to exploring new experiences while also fostering personal growth. She understood that she craved emotional intimacy and sought comfort in vulnerability. She described her ideal partner as someone who shared her passion for travel and valued intentionality in relationships.

After embracing this newfound clarity, Sarah started dating again but with a more discerning eye. She began engaging with individuals who aligned more closely with her blueprint. When she met Alex, they immediately connected due to their shared love of adventure and personal growth. Reflecting on her blueprint during this budding relationship helped Sarah navigate challenges with confidence and intentionality. By sticking to her core values, goals, and emotional needs, Sarah was ultimately able to build the fulfilling partnership she desired.

Another compelling example is David, a 29-year-old graphic designer. After a string of short-lived, unfulfilling relationships, David felt the need to identify and redefine what he sought in love. He began his blueprint by listing his core values, which included creativity, connection, and support. In exploring his emotional needs, he realized that he wanted to feel understood and valued in his partnerships. David's goal was to build a lasting relationship while embracing his individuality.

Through this reflective exercise, David recognized that he often gravitated toward partners who stifled his creative identity. He detailed his ideal partner as someone who encouraged him to pursue his passions while also sharing interests in art and culture. This newfound understanding of himself allowed David to engage more authentically with others and articulate his desires clearly.

When he met Mia, a fellow graphic designer with similar values and passions, David felt empowered to communicate openly from the beginning. They shared mutual respect for one another's independence, fostering a healthy relationship built on creativity, laughter, and emotional safety. By adhering to the principles laid out in his blueprint, David enjoyed a relationship that aligned seamlessly with his aspirations.

As you reflect on your own relationship journey, it's valuable to consider vulnerability as an essential cornerstone of authentic connection. Vulnerability opens the door to deeper emotional intimacy and understanding. It's about daring to share your true self with another person, even when it feels uncertain or intimidating. This notion is beautifully illustrated in the experiences of individuals who embraced their vulnerability as they sought to build their relationship blueprints.

Consider the insights of Lisa, who had spent years building walls around her heart. After creating her blueprint, she recognized that her longing for connection often clashed with her tendency to guard her emotions. Through her reflections, she understood that she needed to let go of her fears of rejection and begin opening up. This shift in perspective guided Lisa to approach relationships with greater authenticity.

When she met Tom, an individual who matched her commitment to personal growth, Lisa was frank about her past experiences and vulnerabilities. By sharing her blueprint and her desire for openness, Lisa allowed Tom to respond with equal honesty. Their relationship blossomed through shared vulnerability, empowering both of them in ways they had never anticipated. Lisa's journey into vulnerability transformed not only her connection with Tom but also her own understanding of love.

As you embark on the creation of your relationship blueprint, hold space for your own stories of struggle, growth, and discovery. Allow yourself the freedom to explore your unique path, reflecting on the lessons learned along the way. This journey is not simply a checklist of qualities but a living document that evolves with you. Your blueprint should invite flexibility, embracing the understanding that relationships require ongoing effort and adaptation.

Throughout this process, you may also want to identify the intentions you wish to carry forth in your relationships. Consider creating mindful affirmations that reinforce your values, goals, and emotional needs. By repeating these affirmations regularly, you can solidify your commitment to yourself and your vision, empowering your path forward.

As your blueprint develops, remember to share your insights with potential partners. Openness about your values and aspirations fosters transparency, smoothing the way for authentic connections. By communicating what you seek in relationships, you set clear expectations and encourage others to share their visions as well.

To further enhance your relationship blueprint, it may be useful to seek feedback from trusted friends or loved ones. Sharing your reflections with those who know you deeply could provide valuable insights, and they may see aspects of your journey that you hadn't considered. This support can reinforce your aspirations and inspire you as you continue to evolve.

Ultimately, the journey of creating your relationship blueprint nurtures self-awareness and intentionality. As you reflect on your values, goals, emotional needs, and the type of partner you desire, you equip yourself with the knowledge necessary to navigate the complexities of love.

This empowered perspective fosters agency, ensuring that you enter relationships with clarity, understanding, and confidence.

With your blueprint as a guiding light, visualize the partnership you long to create. Imagine yourself surrounded by love and support, embracing the richness of your connection. Trust in the process and the intentionality you've cultivated. The effort you put into crafting your relational framework will pay off, as it guides your actions and choices in the realm of love.

Creating your relationship blueprint is a transformative experience, guiding you toward authentic relationships filled with love, mutual respect, and understanding. By engaging in reflective exercises and intentional planning, you unlock the potential to nurture connections that align with your most heartfelt desires. Embrace the journey with openness, and let your blueprint illuminate your path to a fulfilling and enriched relationship journey.

The Journey Ahead

As we reach the conclusion of our exploration into the multifaceted world of love and marriage, let's take a moment to reflect on the remarkable journey that lies ahead for each of us. The road to authentic love and fulfilling relationships is one that requires courage, introspection, and a willingness to evolve. It is not merely a destination, but rather an ever-unfolding adventure filled with opportunities for growth, understanding, and emotional connection.

The themes we've covered throughout this book

remind us that relationships are complex, woven from a fabric of societal expectations, personal experiences, emotional needs, and the profound desire for connection. Yet, it is essential to recognize that the pursuit of genuine love is not just about finding a partner; it is also about deepening our relationship with ourselves.

In our rapid-paced world, it can be easy to lose sight of the profound significance that love brings to our lives. As we engage in a journey toward self-discovery, we must remain committed to understanding our needs, desires, and the values we cherish. The pursuit of authentic love demands that we look inward, that we cultivate emotional intelligence and awareness, and that we are willing to learn from both our successes and our failures.

Continuous learning is a vital aspect of this journey. Love, much like life itself, is not a linear path; it is filled with twists, turns, and unexpected detours. Each experience provides us with insights—each heartbreak, a lesson learned; each moment of joy, a reminder of what is possible. As we navigate the complexities of relationships, it is crucial to remain open to the lessons that they offer. We should approach each encounter, whether it brings happiness or sorrow, as a teacher, one that enriches our understanding of love and connection.

Imagine standing at the threshold of a new chapter in your life—whether it be the beginning of a romantic relationship, the strengthening of an existing bond, or even the brave decision to step back and invest in your own self-care. It is within these moments that we must embrace the uncertainties, for they hold the potential for tremendous growth. However, we cannot move forward without reflecting on where we have been.

To foster this growth, we must allow ourselves the grace of introspection. Begin by asking yourself: What have I learned from my past relationships? What patterns do I recognize in my interactions with others? Understanding the answers to these questions lays the groundwork for a healthier approach to future connections. It highlights our emotional needs and helps us identify red flags, ensuring that we do not repeat detrimental patterns that may have caused pain before.

Moreover, embracing vulnerability is essential on this journey. Love is inherently risky; it requires us to show up authentically, to wear our hearts on our sleeves. We must be brave enough to express our true selves, to share our fears and aspirations with those we hold dear. It is this openness that fosters deeper emotional bonds. Vulnerability paves the way for authentic connections; it invites others to reciprocate, creating an environment where mutual trust can flourish.

As you move forward, consider the importance of compassion—towards yourself and towards others. We are all imperfect beings, navigating our own labyrinths of emotions, insecurities, and hopes. In moments of conflict or misunderstanding, practice empathy. Seek to understand rather than to judge, both yourself and your partner. This approach nurtures a forgiving atmosphere, allowing relationships to heal and grow rather than stagnate.

In contemplating the future of love, remember that it is okay to redefine what love means to you. Our definitions of love are shaped by culture, upbringing, and personal experience. As society evolves, so too should our understanding of love and relationships. Embrace the idea that love is not a rigid construct; rather, it can take on many forms—each as valid and beautiful as the next. Challenge traditional notions of commitment, exploring what partnership looks like in the modern world.

As we tread down this path, we should not only focus on romantic love. The journey encompasses a broader spectrum of connections—friendships, family bonds, and platonic relationships, all of which are equally significant in our quest for fulfillment. Each of these relationships teaches us invaluable lessons about trust, loyalty, and understanding, shaping our capacity for deeper emotional connectivity.

Acknowledge the power of community. Relationships thrive in a supportive environment, where individuals bolster one another and share their experiences. As we individually embark on our journeys, we must strive to cultivate connections that reflect respect, encouragement, and shared wisdom. Recognize that you are not alone; countless others are on parallel journeys, seeking love, understanding, and commitment. Building supportive networks can enhance your experience, providing a buffer during challenging times while amplifying your joyous moments.

Engaging with others who share your desire for authentic connections fosters accountability. Discuss your aspirations and vulnerabilities, and be open to feedback. Through community engagement, you will discover that your experiences are not isolated, providing comfort in the realization that many share your quest for genuine love.

This collective experience nurtures empathy, allowing you to understand different perspectives and appreciate the complexities of love across various contexts.

As you venture forth into this exploration of love and relationships, take heed of the importance of balance. The interplay between giving and receiving is integral to healthy partnerships. To truly connect with another, we must learn to open ourselves to receive love just as much as we give it. It is a dance of mutuality, where each partner contributes equally to the sustenance of the relationship. An imbalance can lead to resentment or emotional fatigue, so embrace the collaborative nature of love.

Moreover, continually nurture your individuality within your partnerships. While it is crucial to build a shared life, it is equally important to foster your own identity. Both partners should prioritize their growth and passions, exploring interests that bring joy independent of the relationship. This not only enriches your life but invigorates your connection, as both individuals can bring their unique experiences and insights into the partnership.

Reflect on the moments that ignite your spirit, the activities that nourish your soul. Whether it's pursuing a hobby, engaging with nature, or investing time in self-reflection, prioritize these elements in your life. This dedication to self-care translates to stronger, healthier relationships, enhancing your ability to invest in love authentically.

As the passage of time reveals its lessons, you will begin to notice changes in your conception of love and connection. The answers you seek may not be clear-cut;

instead, embrace the gray areas that life often presents. Trust the process, knowing that clarity will come with time and experience. Acknowledge that it is entirely normal to reassess your desires as you grow; relationships evolve, and so do the people within them.

Perhaps you will find that your vision for your future relationship has shifted. Allow these changes to be a guiding light rather than a source of fear. The more you embrace the evolving nature of love, the more equipped you will be to foster meaningful connections that align with your true self. Trust in your ability to discern your core values and priorities within relationships; they are pivotal in shaping a life filled with authenticity.

Let us not forget that love is both a journey and a destination. It asks us to be engaged, to work diligently, and to invest in our relationships continually. In doing so, we transform ourselves and the bonds we share with others into something truly remarkable. Acknowledge that each step—no matter how small—on this journey holds value. Celebrate your milestones, learn from challenges, and savor the moments of joy that arise as you cultivate deeper connections.

As we conclude this exploration, remember that your journey is uniquely yours. Embrace every twist and turn, as they serve to enrich your understanding of love and relationships. Step boldly into the future, equipped with knowledge and self-awareness. Allow the lessons of empathy, vulnerability, and authenticity to guide your steps, and trust that love, in all its forms, will find you when you remain open to it.

In this vast world, we are bound together by the shared experience of seeking connection. As you embark on your journey ahead, know that you possess the power to build the love you desire—a love based not on convenience or obligation, but on genuine affection, understanding, and respect. Let your heart lead the way as you navigate the ever-unfolding tapestry of love that awaits you.

Thanks for Joining the Ride!

Wow, here we are at the finish line, and what a ride it has been! Thank you, dear reader, for joining me on this wild trek through the intriguing world of modern marriage and relationships. I hope you've uncovered as many eye-opening insights as I have along the way! From challenging societal norms in chapters like "The Marriage Mirage" to recognizing the vital importance of authenticity in "Building Authentic Connections", I truly believe you're now equipped with a new lens through which to view love and commitment.

As we navigated through the tumultuous waters of motivations behind marriage, it became clear that understanding these hidden forces isn't just enlightening; it empowers you to make more informed choices in your own journey of love. I hope this book has sparked that burning curiosity within you, leading you to reflect on your own relationships in a more profound way. Remember, love is meant to be real, deep, and dynamic—so take those insights and let them fuel your passion for true connection!

Life is far too short to settle for anything less than what you deserve. This book was designed to inspire you to challenge your assumptions, dive bravely into communication, and be the architect of a relationship filled with genuine love. I can't stress enough—your voice matters in your relationship journey! So don't hesitate to express your thoughts, your needs, and your desires. That's how authentic connections are built!

As you close these pages, I encourage you to hold onto the lessons learned and to keep asking questions.

Engage with your partner, revisit those thought-provoking questions we touched on, and remember that growth within a relationship is an ongoing adventure. Honor your unique journey, consider the lessons of those who've walked the path before you, and don't shy away from embracing the complexities of love.

In the end, this isn't just about surviving marriage; it's about thriving together! Embrace your individuality while fostering that beautiful partnership you've always dreamed of. Let this book serve as your trusty guide, helping you explore the ever-evolving nature of relationships. Go on, take what you've learned here and let it illuminate your path forward. The future of your love life can be breathtakingly beautiful—it just needs your heart and wisdom to fully blossom!

With heartfelt gratitude and excitement for your journey,

Pheladi Anastacia Thaba